THE
ETHICAL
PSYCHIC

THE
ETHICAL
PSYCHIC

JENNIFER LISA VEST, PhD

North Atlantic Books
Huichin, unceded Ohlone land
aka Berkeley, California

Published by
North Atlantic Books
Huichin, unceded Ohlone land
aka Berkeley, California

Cover art © hanakaz via Getty Images
Cover design by Jess Morphew
Book design by Happenstance Type-O-Rama

Printed in the United States of America

The Ethical Psychic: A Beginner's Guide to Healing with Integrity, Avoiding Unethical Encounters, and Using Your Gifts for Good is sponsored and published by North Atlantic Books, an educational nonprofit based in the unceded Ohlone land Huichin (*aka* Berkeley, CA) that collaborates with partners to develop cross-cultural perspectives; nurture holistic views of art, science, the humanities, and healing; and seed personal and global transformation by publishing work on the relationship of body, spirit, and nature.

North Atlantic Books' publications are distributed to the US trade and internationally by Penguin Random House Publisher Services. For further information, visit our website at www.northatlanticbooks.com.

Library of Congress Cataloging-in-Publication Data

Names: Vest, Jennifer Lisa, author.
Title: The ethical psychic : a beginner's guide to healing with integrity, avoiding unethical encounters, and using your gifts for good / by Jennifer Lisa Vest, Ph.D.
Description: Berkeley, California : North Atlantic Books, [2022] | Includes bibliographical references and index.
Identifiers: LCCN 2022003238 | ISBN 9781623177386 (trade paperback) | ISBN 9781623177393 (ebook)
Subjects: LCSH: Psychics. | Ethics.
Classification: LCC BF1040 .V47 2022 | DDC 130—dc23/eng/20220224
LC record available at https://lccn.loc.gov/2022003238

1 2 3 4 5 6 7 8 9 KPC 26 25 24 23 22

For my mother,
Michele (MIKE-ul) Lee Davis,

who was a psychic
before it was OK to be one

and who warned me
about the dangers of this work.

I was listening, Mom.

And it harms none, do what ye will

—WITCHES' REDE

CONTENTS

PREFACE xi

INTRODUCTION 1

1 THE TRAITS OF AN ETHICAL PSYCHIC. 9

Trait #1: Being of Service 11
Trait #2: Being Authentic. 13
Trait #3: Being Self-Aware. 29
Trait#4: Learning from Mistakes and Being Humble. 31
Trait #5: Being Sensitive to Client Needs 36
Trait #6: Listening to a Higher Source. 40

2 THE RISKS OF PSYCHIC WORK. 47

Unethical Risk #1: Invading the Privacy of Others. 48
Unethical Risk #2: Client Dependency 51
Unethical Risk #3: Financial Exploitation 55
Unethical Risk #4: Making Matters Worse 58

3 INTERFERING WITH THE WILL OF OTHERS. 65

Unethical Risk #5: Perverting the Will of Another 66
Unethical Risk #6: The Misuse of Sexual Energy 74
Fake Gurus 80

4 WORKING WITH SPIRITS AND SOUL PATHS 89

Unethical Risk # 7: Controlling the Destiny of Souls 90
Unethical Risk #8: Creating Disharmony through
                Portals and Possession 96

5 HOW TO BECOME AN ETHICAL PSYCHIC **103**

Choose Teachers Carefully 103
Choose Colleagues Carefully 107
Examine Your Motives 107
Do the Emotional Work...............................108
Dedicate Yourself to Becoming a Hollow Bone.......... 112
Live a Balanced Life 115

6 FREQUENTLY ASKED QUESTIONS **117**

ACKNOWLEDGMENTS **151**

NOTES **157**

INDEX...................................... **165**

ABOUT THE AUTHOR **173**

PREFACE

I began writing this guidebook in the second month of 2017, less than two weeks after the inauguration of one of the most unpopular presidents in United States history. The country was in turmoil. Record numbers of people were taking to the street to protest and a majority of the population was concerned that we were in the midst of a moral turning point. The greatest critique being made of the US president and his cabinet in 2017 was neither a political nor a policy critique—it was a moral one. The world was terrified by the possible consequences that could result from a presidency that lacked moral standards.

At this time I was teaching a class called Conscious Psychic, which I first began teaching in 2012, in my living room, to a handful of students under the title, Develop Your Sixth Sense to Shift Your Consciousness. I would explain to my students that my class was different from other psychic development classes because I wasn't just teaching them how to develop their gifts, I was teaching them how to develop their gifts in service to the planet. As such, I frequently spoke about ethics. Some of my students groaned and complained about this frequent emphasis. Others just chalked it up to old habits dying hard. I was, after all, a former Professor of Philosophy who had taught ethics to college students for many years. Maybe I just couldn't help myself. While some students appreciated the ethical content, others tired of it and went in search of easygoing teachers who would teach them how to cast spells and other self-serving skills.

Over the years, I had the misfortune of seeing some of my spellcasting former students turn to filthy magic or the "dark arts" and other abusive psychic practices. They had rebelled against my teachings because I had often warned against pursuing such practices. Their decision to jettison ethics resulted in exactly what I had cautioned against. This confirmed my belief that teaching students how to be ethical psychics was of paramount importance.

Over the years I have taught a number of courses in the psychic and healing arts including Mediumship, Medical Intuition, Reiki, Intuitive Healing Energetics, Akashic Records, and others. In each of these, I emphasized the importance of ethics, and as time went on, I became convinced of the need to collect all of my teachings into a book.

A person can be gifted but use their gifts in an unethical manner. This book will address this problem and provide ethical guidelines. Psychically gifted persons have a responsibility to those without gifts. There are limits as to how psychic gifts should be employed. Just because a person can read someone's mind doesn't mean they should. It is not ethical to use one's psychic gifts to seduce. And while there is nothing wrong with making large sums of money using one's psychic gifts, there are conditions that must be met when doing so.

In recent years, there has been an increase in the number of people claiming to have psychic (psi) gifts and wanting to develop or share them. At the same time, interest in all topics related to psi has grown. More and more people consult psychics, mediums, medical intuitives, life coaches, spiritual advisors, and healers. Increasingly, people are leaving traditional religions to join nondenominational spiritual bodies. More and more people are also using integrative and holistic health practitioners, and there has been a surge in interest in books published on esoteric and psi topics.

People are bringing their most pressing life and health problems to psychically gifted practitioners of various kinds instead of to establishment Western healers. This is evidence of a planetary shift in consciousness. So many factors are coming together now: the planetary shift in consciousness, political upheaval, the increased codependent needs of the general population, and an increase in the number of light workers developing their gifts. Now is the time. All of these factors make it more important than ever that psychics behave ethically and that standards be established for psychic work.

How does the average psychic learn how to be ethical? I teach my students how to be ethical, but my classes cannot reach the growing number of light workers developing every day. This guidebook was written to assist the many aspiring and practicing psychics in taking special care in how they practice their craft so they might assist in the global shift in consciousness.

INTRODUCTION

I wonder how many young bucks today qualify to become medicine [people]. They think in terms of glory. It is not glorious. That is not how I see it—it requires many sacrifices . . . it is not a glory thing and it is nothing to brag about.

—PETER S. CATCHES, LAKOTA MEDICINE MAN

Psychic gifts, like other talents, can be used for positive or negative purposes. Just because a person has psychic gifts doesn't mean they are spiritually evolved. Throughout history, people in a variety of cultures have feared psychics (or supersensory persons) for good reason. There have always been people who have used their gifts to overpower others. Some people knowingly use their gifts for ill; some people harm others with their gifts through ignorance. A supersensory person who is not ethical can and often does cause harm. And a psychic who does not intentionally decide to be ethical will very often fail to be ethical. As one well-known twentieth century psychic explained it: "ESP is a will instrument. All persons having strong wills have a greater capacity to call forth ESP powers. If the will is forceful or selfishly designed, ESP becomes an instrument of destruction."[1]

Magicians, charlatans, and fraudsters of various types have often used the pretended display of otherworldly gifts to separate gullible people from their money. And even those who have genuine gifts are sometimes tempted to misuse or exaggerate them in order to make money. Others have used their abilities for more nefarious purposes—to control others or to unfairly gain advantage over those who lack supersensory abilities.

In traditional Indigenous cultures throughout the world, instruction in supersensory arts has always been accompanied by instructions for how to be a good person, a good healer, shaman, or medicine person. In the twenty-first-century, non-tribal Western world, most psychics do not get this training, nor do they have the benefit of a dedicated teacher. Instead, developing psychics must often acquire the knowledge they need on their own—by seeking out teachers, courses, and books to enlarge their understanding of their gifts. Because many psychics are self-taught, they are often working without the benefit of instruction in psychical ethics. It is not enough for psychics to learn how to maximize the efficacy of their psychic gifts. They must also learn how to use their gifts for good and never for harm. They must learn how to be ethical psychics.

WHY WE NEED THIS BOOK

We are currently living in a shift in consciousness where time is speeding up, people are stepping more firmly onto their paths, more and more people are being born with gifts, and there is greater societal acceptance for the expression of these gifts. This is a good thing. But it means that there is a mad rush to learn and to learn fast. Most students are no longer learning in the context of long apprenticeships; they are no longer even seeking face-to-face instruction with revered teachers; they are no longer living in their communities or talking to their elders. Then too, students are interested in learning about the psychic traditions found in communities and cultures outside of their own. So much transplantation and mixing has occurred between communities and parts of the world that some students don't belong to any one culture or community—they belong to many. Given these circumstances, students have a real need to obtain access to teachings that will help them to develop their gifts in a positive way. While many books exist about how to develop psychic gifts, there is scant mention of ethics in these books and few books are devoted exclusively to this topic. This book addresses this critical void.

WHAT IS AN ETHICAL PSYCHIC?

Ethics is the field of philosophy that is concerned with a critical consideration of moral beliefs. As such, it includes a critical and reflective assessment of our beliefs about questions such as "What are the traits of a good person?" and "What is the right thing to do?" This book is concerned with the questions "What are the traits of a good psychic?" and "What is the right thing to do with one's psychic gifts?" An ethical psychic endeavors to be a good person and to do the right thing in his or her practice. An ethical psychic is intentional and conscious in her use of her gifts; she strives to use her gifts to help and never harm, and she takes steps to ensure that no negative consequences result from the expression of her gifts. An ethical psychic does not just seek to do no harm; he consciously and carefully examines all of the possible effects of his work and makes decisions about how to work according to these reflections, doing everything in his power to ensure a positive outcome.

Despite his archaic use of language which equates black with bad and white with good, we can learn from famed scholar of esoterica Manly P. Hall's definitions of magic in our discernment between ethical and unethical psychics. Hall writes, "The black magician's motto is 'might is right' (survival of the fittest). The white magician's motto is 'right is might' (survival of all) . . . Motive is the key to the problem of magic. Even the greatest of white magicians can become a degenerate in an instant if his motives become unworthy. The white magician serves humanity; the black magician seeks to serve himself."[2]

WHO THIS BOOK IS FOR

This book is meant to be a resource for all psychics and healers but especially for those supersensory persons who have not benefited from long study with master teachers who might have provided them with a strong ethical foundation for the practice of their gifts. It is also for students who have teachers. This book is not meant to be a substitution for learning ethics from a teacher. It is meant as an adjunct resource.

It is also my hope that the beginning psychic who is developing her craft on her own by reading books and watching videos will come across this book and find it useful for her development, and that the beginning psychic or healer will decide after reading this book that they should work with a teacher. This book will also help that student to choose the right teacher.

This book is also meant for teachers. It is my hope that teachers of psychic and healing arts can use this as a type of course book for their classes. Both beginning and intermediate courses of psychic instruction would benefit by including this book in their curriculum.

Because I am a psychic, a medium, a medical intuitive, an energy healer, and an Akashic Records reader, I include examples from all of these practices. Thus, this book is versatile and can be used by teachers and classes teaching a wide variety of intuitive arts. It is my hope too that this book will be of use to those individuals who are either in a spiritual community or are thinking about starting one. They can obtain some guidance in this text about how to avoid the unethical behaviors that can lead to the creation of communities centered on fake gurus.

This book provides much needed information for developing psychics and their teachers. In it, the reader will find a description of the traits of an ethical psychic, the unethical risks entailed in doing psychic work, best practices, and a list of frequently asked questions. People who are conscious of the risks entailed in this work, who are determined to develop the traits of an ethical psychic, and who engage in the best practices outlined in this book will become ethical psychics.

ABOUT MY SPIRITUAL LINEAGE

As a healer and ceremonialist, trained in numerous traditions (medical intuition, Reiki, Akashic Records, past life regression, and mediumship), my work is informed by my particular cultural and spiritual lineages. I was trained in the traditions of African American Hoodoo, Native American sweat lodge, Jamaican Revivalism, and Trinidadian Shango and spiritualism; in addition, I have studied multiple healing modalities such as Reiki, Pranic Healing, spiritual healing, and quantum healing hypnosis technique (QHHT).

I come from a long line of seers. On my maternal line, my mother, grandmother, and great-grandmother had psychic gifts. My mother identified me early as the one in my generation with the gifts. On my paternal side, my grandfather and great-grandparents also had the gift of sight. When I was an infant, my great-grandmother on my paternal line, Lula-Mae, identified me as the one who would carry the gift into the next generation. She began training me as a child and continued to teach me after her death, taking me to school in the Other World at night throughout my youth and into my thirties.

Born with the gifts of clairvoyance, clairaudience, clairsentience, and mediumship, I was able to develop these gifts through long study and practice at the hands of many teachers. I studied informally with several women healers in the Jamaican Revivalist and Trinidadian Shango traditions (including Mother Joyce, Sister Nelson, Mother Barrett, Queenie, Sister Grant, Mother Mavis, Mother Viola, Mother Wright, Mother Robinson and others), and I was trained as a firekeeper in the Native American sweat lodge by Phoenix Bennett. I also learned a great deal from my Seminole and Muskogee "aunties and uncles," Don Little Cloud Davenport, Bonita Sizemore, Bojack, Millie Kecheshawno, and Zenobia Embry—founders of the Black Native American Association of Oakland.

As a child, I used to attend many churches and mosques and I spent a great deal of time having long conversations with religious leaders. I went to Black Spiritualist churches such as the Church of God in Christ and Spiritual Baptist churches where I was able to see the Holy Ghost come into the churches and take over the bodies of the Mothers/anointed ones. I talked at length to the Mothers and learned a lot from them. I also benefited immensely from my time spent with two Islamic professors, Abidullah and Tasneema Ghazi (one of whom I worked for as an editor of Islamic books between the ages of fourteen and fifteen); a Methodist minister, Reverend Killian; and a Presbyterian minister, Reverend Q. Gerald Roseberry, among others.

I also studied with veteran mediums and healers in the white spiritualist tradition at Cassadaga Spiritualist Camp in Cassadaga, Florida, where I took classes in psychic development, mediumship, healing, and trance for five years with such teachers as Maeda Jones, Mary Rose Gray, Marie Wilson-Gates, Joan Piper, and Suzanne DeWees, among others. I became a Reiki Master under the Reiki Master Marie Gates in the Usui tradition descended from Takata. I have also taken classes in Pranic Healing with Master Choa, transformational hypnosis, and other modalities. I spent ten years undergoing past life regressions in order to develop an understanding of the impact past lives have on current lives and then was trained by Dolores Cannon to conduct past life regressions and healings using the QHHT. I am a former professor of Cross-Cultural Philosophy where my areas of specialization were African and Native American philosophy, and I completed a master's thesis on women healers in Jamaica based on extensive oral interviews with dozens of healers.

I have participated in many ceremonies in Revivalism, Pocomania, Shango, and Vodun, and have also participated in Native American sweat lodges, Native American pipe ceremonies, and others. I have belonged to many Hoodoo and Women of Color ceremonial circles and I have started many spiritual circles and BIPOC (Black, Indigenous, and People of Color) performative arts organizations in a variety of communities related to my training. I started a Medical Intuition circle and a Psychic Detective circle in my home, and I have participated in Trance circles. I have a PhD in Indigenous Philosophies and Ethnic Studies from UC Berkeley where I completed a dissertation on African and Native American epistemologies. I worked as a professor for ten years and developed courses on African, Caribbean, African American, and Native American philosophy, and I have published papers and delivered numerous lectures and keynotes on these topics.

My entire life I have been guided and taught by Spirit Teachers who, when I was a child, would come and get me at night and take me to spirit school on the Other Side. As I got older, my guides began to take me to the past and the future and to other countries. Throughout my life they have taught me as much as my human teachers have, and they have led me to the appropriate human teachers at the appropriate times. Much of what I do as a teacher and a healer is guided by the information I receive from them directly through channeling or divine inspiration, mysticism, or in ceremony.

As a mixed blood of Haitian, Seminole, African American, Cherokee, German, and Norwegian heritage, I combine what I have learned from African, Caribbean, and Native American Spiritism traditions and Afro-American and Euro-American Spiritualist traditions into my practice. In all that I do, I am guided by Spirit and I do my best to be a pure vessel and a hollow bone.

THE TRAITS OF AN
ETHICAL PSYCHIC

*Our behavior must be the best. I do not argue, do not fight, do not
hate, do not gossip, and I have never said a swear word. I have
not chased after women and I have controlled my lust for them. I
have never touched a woman patient other than was necessary to
cure or heal them.*[1]

—FOOLS CROW, OGLALA LAKOTA HOLY MAN

While developing their gifts, a psychic can also develop their character. People of good character make good psychics, but being a
good person will not automatically make you a good psychic. It is
necessary to develop self-awareness, reflect on your character, and
think about the character traits that a good psychic/healer ought
to have or develop. Only by developing certain traits alongside
your gift can you become an ethical psychic.

In traditional Indigenous cultures, character has always been
central to the choice of healers. Medicine people, shamans, priest-
esses, and the like are not chosen only because of their raw skill,
but because they are good people, with good intentions, who think
carefully about others and strive to always help those who are in

need of healing. In the modern West, healers choose themselves rather than waiting for a community to choose them. It is now up to these self-chosen healers to endeavor to develop a healing character.

SIX KEY CHARACTER TRAITS THAT DEFINE AN ETHICAL PSYCHIC

1. Being motivated by service

2. Being authentic

3. Being self-aware

4. Being able to acknowledge and learn from mistakes

5. Being sensitive to a client's needs

6. Being guided by something larger than yourself

TRAIT #1: BEING OF SERVICE

Among the most important traits that a good psychic ought to have is a dedication to service. When we share our psychic gifts in an effort to help others, this is the best use of our gifts. Spiritualist psychic-medium Jesse James Jr. felt that the whole purpose of his having gifts was to be of service. "To me, service is the greatest religion," he explains. "There is no religion greater than service. That should be the path of everybody."[2]

If we have a dedication to using our gifts to serve others and we make decisions about how to practice with this central goal in mind, we are less likely to harm our clients. There are many occupations where service is the central goal. Teachers, therapists, social workers, founders of nonprofits, and some nurses, doctors, and elected officials are often guided by a desire to serve. The psychic healer should be likewise motivated.

When motivated by a desire to serve, you bring a certain clarity of focus to your work. When making decisions about who to work with and for, always ask yourself if these decisions will help you serve better or help you serve more people. If you do this each time, you will invariably make the right decision. If, on the other hand, you make business decisions about the practice of your gifts without taking into account how they will affect your ability to serve others, you risk engaging in activities that are harmful.

Suppose you are invited to do readings at a fair or an event and there is a good chance you will be able to give twenty readings in one day. This sounds like a great way to help twenty people and make money in doing so. But then what if the organizer of the fair takes you aside and explains to you that he wants you to tell all your clients that they have soul wounds. "Just throw the word into your readings once or twice. No big deal," he instructs you. He sells a service called "soul wound recovery" and wants you to prime these clients to sign up for his program. You may feel compelled to take the job because 1) it is an opportunity to use your gifts; 2) it is an opportunity to make much-needed money; and 3) it is an opportunity to network with a successful entrepreneur in your field. Because of these compelling reasons, you may be willing to alter your readings slightly to satisfy the organizer's request for a plug. But a psychic motivated by service would be concerned about the implications of giving people false information. What would be the impact of telling your clients they had a soul wound? What would happen to the clients who believed they have a soul wound but could not afford the soul wound recovery therapy? How could you better assist them if you instead focused every minute of the reading on their concerns or gave them information and guidance to improve their life?

Some psychics may tell themselves that the few seconds they take away from their message to plug their colleague's business won't really detract from their message. But the ethical psychic will ask themselves whether they are still being of service to their clients while lying to them. Is it really true that everyone has a soul wound? The psychic will wonder if the work her colleague does with clients is in the clients' best interests. The ethical psychic knows that once you begin promoting another practitioner's work, you become responsible for what they do or do not do for their clients. A practitioner who manipulates the readings of the psychics that work for them in order to increase business is motivated by profits not service.

Examples of situations that will be difficult to navigate without a clear service focus are the following:

1. Being offered highly profitable opportunities to provide services or teach courses you are not fully qualified to offer

2. Being offered large sums of money to work with clients who require mental health services but prefer to come to you for help

3. Being asked to label your services according to the popular trends of a particular culture, place, or time (e.g., shaman,

Akashic Records reader, channeler) despite lacking the necessary training

4. Being asked to be on call twenty-four hours a day or to work with large groups of people, where such work will be exhausting and undermine your effectiveness

5. Being expected to use your psychic abilities for free for family and friends when you are too emotionally invested to provide impartial assistance

When the psychic is motivated by service, competing concerns—financial, cultural, or familial—take a back seat to the psychic protecting her own health, traditions, and values. Having service as a central motivating force ensures that you will not let the influence of others or considerations of money or marketing trump your concerns about the welfare of your clients and maintaining your integrity. This does not mean that you do not account for the marketing and financial needs of your business. It is not necessary to starve in order to be ethical. Instead, you must attenuate your financial motivations with your service motivations, thus ensuring an ethical business practice. Psychic-medium John Edward cautions, "If you choose to give professional readings or even just share your intuitive impressions with those around you, the ethical responsibility is enormous. What you do and say has karmic repercussions and should never be taken lightly or be pursued for any reason other than to help others."[3]

TRAIT #2: BEING AUTHENTIC

Being authentic is key to being an ethical psychic. The importance of being authentic in your work cannot be overstated. An authentic psychic is true to themselves and does not allow circumstances or people to divert them from their purpose. For example, if you believe that your information comes from an ancestor you work with, you do not say you work with Jesus or Archangel Michael when working with Christian clients, nor would you claim to be working with Orishas when working with Caribbean clients. Authenticity is about being true to yourself, true to your spiritual lineage, and true to your purpose.

An authentic psychic will not be easily influenced by fads or popular beliefs. An authentic psychic will not be embarrassed by the information they receive or how they receive it, nor will they censor it to sound more acceptable. As Allison DuBois puts it, "Make no apologies for who you are."[4]

Often, when I am in a session, I get information that, to me, sounds preposterous. When I was first starting out, I used to withhold information that I thought sounded absurd, but over time I learned to trust the information I got no matter how absurd. For example, in one funny medical intuition session I picked up that a woman had a foreign body in her breast. I was really baffled by that until she told me she had breast implants. We both had a good laugh. Another time I was picking up that a surgeon had said some offensive things during a surgery. Since the patient was asleep, how could he have heard them? Turns out he did. I learned the hard way that the "absurd" information was usually the most reliable. Being authentic means being true to yourself, your gift, the information you receive, and how you receive it. When psychics pretend or deny the true nature of their gifts, they are more likely to cause harm to themselves and others.

When I work as a medium, I have a very particular guidance about who I can work with and under what circumstances. This is, in part, because of how I was trained to work as a medium, and it is also, in part, due to what I have learned from the spirits I have brought through and the guidance I have received from my Spirit Teachers. I know that it is not always easy for spirits to come to Earth and talk to the living and that sometimes it interrupts their activities on other planes. I am particular about the types of mediumship sessions I do.

I do not call deceased loved ones of people who are merely curious as to what Uncle Fred is up to. I only conduct mediumship sessions for the purpose of healing extreme situations. This means I specialize in suicides, murders, unexplained deaths, disputes over wills and inheritances that are causing distress for the family, and debilitating grief, especially grief that causes physical or mental health disturbances in the lives of the surviving loved ones.

After years of practice, I have come to a full understanding of what my gifts truly are and how I am meant to use them. It has become clear to me that my primary role is that of healer: a psychic healer or a medium healer. As such, the only time it is appropriate for me to conduct mediumship sessions is when I am certain that my help will be healing for my client. Because my role as a healer includes healing the deceased, my work is limited by the condition that it be healing for both the client and the deceased loved one. It is for this reason that I call specific spirits and I only call them in sessions designed to heal a crisis of some kind.

Other mediums work in other equally important ways that are true to their purposes and their training. For example, many mediums trained in spiritualism are concerned with demonstrating the continuity of life beyond physical death.[5] Such mediums can provide an important teaching to clients by demonstrating the continued existence of their loved ones after death. Learning this can be profoundly transformative for clients and it can be essential to reducing their own fear of death.

Bringing through a loved one can also help people to better understand fate and the choices that people make regarding birth and death. There are many good reasons to be a medium and once a psychic knows what her reason is for doing mediumship, she will be in a position to determine her own authentic way of working.

I once had a potential client who came to me seeking a mediumship session in order to do a family history. I asked him a few questions to determine exactly what he wanted. He said he had a bunch of names but little information about certain family members and wanted to bring those ancestors through to fill in the gaps in his family tree. I chose not to work with him and referred him to a colleague of mine who did not have the same restrictions I had. I had two reasons for not working with this client.

First, he wanted me to bring through a large number of different spirits in one hour. I personally consider that rude. I know how hard it can be for a spirit to come back and to communicate with the living. I don't want to call them here and then dismiss them after a few minutes so I can call in the next spirit. It seems rude in the same way that it would be rude for me to call up my Great Aunt Serilda, invite her over to tea, and then, knowing that it takes her an hour to get properly dressed, an hour to walk to her car, another hour to walk to my front door from her car, I ask her to leave after a fifteen-minute visit so I can invite Cousin Cisco over. It just feels improper to me and it does not fit in with my purpose as a healer of the living *and* the dead.

Now plenty of mediums, including some very famous ones, do talk to large numbers of spirits, one after another, in a short space of time. This is especially the case for those who do *platform mediumship*, in which the purpose is to bring through as many spirits as possible during a set time, in front of a large audience. These mediums are working in this way because their purpose is different than mine. They are able to have a profound effect on a large number of people by showcasing their gift in this way. The purpose of such demonstrations is often to change people's ideas about death. This is a lofty and powerful purpose, but it is not mine. In order to be authentic, I must work in a way consistent with my training, my lineage, and my purpose.

The second reason I could not take the job working with the family historian client was that his reason for calling these relatives forward did not satisfy my criteria of 1) Is it a crisis? or 2) Will it provide profound healing of a physical or mental health issue? The family historian did not *need* to know the details of his great-grandparents' lives in order to heal. He just *wanted* to know. Nothing important—no genetic illnesses, no inheritance issues, no identity dilemmas—were riding on him getting these answers.

Authenticity and Cultural Appropriation

To be authentic, it is important to have clarity about your spiritual lineage, the true nature of your gifts, and the purpose of your gifts. What did you come here to do? What have your teachers taught you? When you know this, you will be in a position to make good decisions about how and when you work, and you can guarantee the authenticity of your work.

Being authentic is arguably an important aspect of any endeavor, but with regard to supersensory work, authenticity is an ethical concern. The primary way in which inauthenticity manifests in the intuitive arts is through rampant cultural appropriation. Many intuitives who lack a grounding in their own culture will pretend to know about other cultures and will then use that pretended knowledge to educate others in order to sell workshops and goods. Cultural appropriation is a wrong that is committed against a whole community, against yourself, and also against your ancestors.

Cultural appropriation is the inauthentic claiming or use of another person's culture for your own gain. To simply practice someone else's culture is not in and of itself cultural appropriation, but when you pretend to be a lineage holder, or when you set yourself up as an expert on someone else's traditions and then receive status or monetary gain from such pretense, you are engaging in cultural appropriation and that is unethical.

There are many examples of this in the modern world. Many non-Indigenous persons now run businesses as shamans, medicine people, and hoodooists. They have so completely appropriated the term *shaman* that many people of color no longer use the term lest they be confused with these practitioners. The entire field of shamanism in the United States has for decades been controlled by prominent European-Americans like Michael Harner, who have altered and repackaged Indigenous traditions for Euro-American consumption.

See, for example, how Harner's Foundation for Shamanic Studies describes his course, *Core Shamanism*:

> *Core shamanism consists of the universal, near-universal, and common features of shamanism, together with journeys to other worlds, a distinguishing feature of shamanism. As originated, researched, and developed by Michael Harner, the principles of core shamanism are not bound to any specific cultural group or perspective. Since the West overwhelmingly lost its shamanic knowledge centuries ago due to religious oppression, the Foundation's programs in core shamanism are particularly intended for Westerners to reacquire access to their rightful spiritual heritage through quality workshops and training courses.[6]*

For many people, neoshamanism or Harnerism (another name for core shamanism) has replaced shamanism. Harner and his students are now considered experts on shamanism. For example, Amazon describes Harner's first book, *The Way of the Shaman*, in the following way, "This classic on shamanism pioneered the modern shamanic renaissance. It is the foremost resource and reference on shamanism." In an online ranking of the "100 Best Shamanism Books of All Time," Harner ranks number one.[7] For many years, they ran the schools and the conferences and wrote the books that were deemed the authoritative texts in the field. They were the keynote speakers at conferences on shamanism. Because they defined and controlled the field for decades, they benefited immensely from their status as "experts."

While there is nothing inherently wrong with white people writing books or teaching classes on Black and Indigenous traditions, and it can be argued that Harner's books and classes have helped many

Americans to have positive transcendent spiritual experiences they might otherwise never have had, his work has also caused harm. The teachings and books of Harner and his students repackage Indigenous practices into detribalized and acultural commodities that displaced and replaced the work of Indigenous shamans.[8] In the wake of a critique of Harnerism, many more books and conferences now feature Indigenous shamans, but neoshamanism provides an important cautionary tale for all psychics and teachers of healing arts.

The problem of cultural appropriation most often manifests as the dominance of "white experts" in spiritual communities and the exclusion of culture-bearers. It is a legacy of conquest and colonialism. For example, the field of sound healing is almost exclusively dominated by European-Americans, despite its origin in Indigenous traditions around the world.[9] We can also look at the practice of yoga, an Indian tradition, which is currently dominated by non-Indian European Americans who run many schools, own many studios, offer many classes, and who are viewed as experts in a practice they imported from another culture. Some of these practitioners were legitimately trained by Indian experts. Some of these practitioners know their lineage and clearly communicate the Indian origins of their practice. But many practitioners have simply become "experts" without acknowledging the origins of their practice. That is cultural appropriation and it is unethical.

The cultural appropriation of African and African American culture is the most pervasive form of cultural appropriation in the US and also the most invisible. For centuries, the absolute subjugation of Africans through enslavement, lynching, continued police brutality, and the outlawing of African customs has made it challenging for Black Americans to retain the African elements of their own culture. People had to hide in the woods to practice African spirituality. Beliefs had to be handed down encoded in song, dance, symbol, and hair styles.

Because of profound anti-Black racism, which is still central in American culture, non-Blacks often refuse to recognize Black culture as culture, and so when Black Americans produce a new cultural form, it is immediately picked up by whites, repackaged, and called by another name. As a result, many Africanisms are not acknowledged or recognized as such.

Elvis Presley was a perfect example of cultural appropriation of Black culture. He went to Black establishments, watched Black singers, and copied their form. Whites were willing to accept the music of Blacks when delivered by whites. Rock and Roll is the product of African musical forms, but many Americans think of it as white. In recent years many white singers have adopted Black soul styles of singing and have made millions singing Black music in white bodies.

The same disturbing phenomena has occurred in the super-sensory community where Hoodoo and Rootwork, developed in African-descended communities, have been appropriated by white herbalists who have redefined Hoodoo as a multicultural tradition or by white witches and pagans who have repackaged elements of Hoodoo as "The Craft." Most recently this appropriation is noticeable on social media platforms, but it has been happening for years.

Writer Chloé Meley explains in *Huck* magazine that although Hoodoo is "a spiritual tradition inspired by West African folklore that was created by enslaved people in the United States[,] on TikTok, . . . the great majority of people making videos about honey jars—a Hoodoo practice used to sweeten up situations and restore relationships with people—are young white witches desperate to reconnect with their ex."[10]

The high levels of cultural appropriation young practitioners are demonstrating today may be a direct result of the decades-long dominance of "white experts" in the field of Hoodoo. One European-American writer wrote several books on Hoodoo and started her own Conjure supply company and her own school, and she became known as an authority in the field. Her books became the references that everyone cited, and she was a highlighted speaker at Hoodoo conferences. She offered courses and certificate programs, and many people bought supplies from her company, despite the fact that she was not from a Hoodoo lineage or community and did not have cultural or spiritual roots in any of the African American or Native American traditions that have contributed to the origins of Hoodoo.

Multicultural journalists Jess Joho and Morgan Sung write about the problem of cultural appropriation in Wicca/witchcraft, explaining,

> *The allure of modern witchcraft lies in the promise that anyone can reclaim their power through a hodgepodge of spiritual mysticism. Yet that mysticism also often borrows from the specific spiritual practices of various oppressed peoples. . . . Aspiring witches must respect the boundaries of closed practices that explicitly state they can only be practiced by people who are descendants of a cultural heritage. Hoodoo, for example, originates from slavery and was created specifically for Black people.[11]*

Culturally appropriating other people's traditions is unethical, and developing psychics must be vigilant in respecting cultural boundaries and lineages. As a mixed-race practitioner with multiple lineages who has trained in several traditions, I am aware that cultures are not always discrete and they do mix. However, I am always careful to only teach from the heritages I am trained in. For example, for a number of years I ran a Women of Color medicine series that involved monthly Cereclasses (*Cereclass* is a term I invented to refer to a hybrid event that combines ceremony and teaching). I conducted Cereclasses on different topics each month to a very diverse class of BIPOC women. I taught from my training in Indigenous, African American, and Caribbean traditions but also sought to include information from other traditions in an effort to include material relevant to all the women present. Whenever I spoke about traditions I was not directly trained in, I was humble and acknowledged the limitation of my knowledge about them. I also made a point of asking self-identified culture-bearers in the room to correct me or to share their own authentic experiences with the tradition.

For example, in talking about ancestor reverence in different cultures, I spoke about joss paper, then invited my Chinese and Vietnamese students to explain the tradition to the class. I would not put anyone on the spot, but I would simply open up the discussion to welcome input from anyone with cultural knowledge about a tradition we were discussing.

On another occasion I decided to celebrate *Diá de los Muertos* (Day of the Dead) in my Cereclass since the class fell on Halloween. As I am not a bearer of Mexican culture, I invited my Mexican and Chicana apprentices to set up the altar, decorate the room, and tell stories about the holiday. I spoke about my related knowledge of Caribbean ancestor altars, which had some similarities. I did not pretend to be an expert on Diá de Los Muertos and I was explicit in acknowledging that it was not a part of my authentic experience or training.

Being respectful of other people's traditions is not difficult, but it does require humility. As such, it does require giving up epistemic authority temporarily. Asking your students to teach you and the other students implies you are not the absolute authority. Some teachers find this challenging. Some spiritual teachers can get caught up in the idea of being the absolute authority for their students. A teacher concerned with cultural appropriation will have to admit what she does not know when she does not know it. The healer will also need to be willing to be criticized and corrected when talking about someone else's culture.

Just because you are an established teacher or ceremonialist in one tradition does not mean you are an authority in all traditions. If a person who has grown up in a tradition wants to correct you, you should welcome the critique.

EXAMPLES OF AUTHENTICITY AND CULTURAL APPROPRIATION

1. If you are not Indigenous/First Nations, do not claim to be a Native healer, medicine person, sweat lodge leader, *kahuna,* and so on.

2. If you have not completed training in a given modality, do not call yourself by that name—that is, do not say you are a Reiki Master, a Pranic healer or a past life regressionist if you have only dabbled in these fields.

3. If you are providing energy healing to a client, and they ask you for messages, but you have not been trained to receive mediumistic messages, tell the client the truth and do not attempt to give them messages.

4. If you have not been trained in how to run a particular type of ceremony (sweat lodge, Ayahuasca, peyote, exorcism, etc.), do not do so or claim to be able to do so.

5. If you work with nature spirits, devas, ancestors, or spirit guides, do not claim to work with other beings just because other people do or because your clients or students have an interest in them.

6. Do not allow people to misattribute your gifts. For example, if a colleague tells a potential client you are a powerful shaman but you are not trained as a shaman, be sure to correct this mistake.

Ethical Culture Sharing

Cultural appropriation should not be confused with culture sharing. We live in a polyglot world and, in the US, we combine many cultures. Also, mixed persons (like myself) necessarily combine traditions. The practice of cultural appropriation is usually committed by persons in the dominant culture of a society and the motive is usually to achieve financial or status rewards. Learning from other cultures and combining traditions is not inherently problematic, but when such practices are exercised with arrogance and inauthentic claims of authority, the learning turns into exploiting.

Because of my varied background, I have sometimes found it to be the case that I cannot recall where I learned something. Also, I have relatives and ancestors who were incapable of identifying the traditions we came from. They might have just said, "We do things this way" or "This is a Vest trait." Sometimes it was only by immersing myself in ancestral cultures that I was able to identify certain traits as belonging to certain cultures I am descended from. For the Native who is adopted, or relocated, for the immigrant or refugee, for the descendant of enslaved people, it is a challenge to know one's heritage. Studying the traditions of the people you believe to be your people is not cultural appropriation. Learning from the next best thing—that is, finding elders in an adjacent tradition—is not cultural appropriation. Seeking to honor your ancestors by reclaiming lost traditions you did not grow up with is not cultural appropriation. Many of us who were raised in the cultures where our spiritual traditions come from have sought to learn more about our traditions so that we can practice them with authenticity.

Dr. Erika Buenaflor, a modern-day *curandera* and *curanderismo* scholar, explains,

> *Researching and understanding how the ancient Yucatec Maya and Mexica conducted fire limpia rites greatly deepened the sacrality of the fire limpias I offered. The level of faith of both the curandera/o and participant always correlates with how effective it will be. By equipping myself with the sacred meanings and practices of my rich history and culture, I became more*

grounded in and comfortable with these rites. I also began to put into practice nuanced ancient understandings and methods, particularly the knowledge that all the tools used have a soul essence. I learned how to work with these entities and for what purposes.[12]

Dr. Buenaflor did not assume that because she was Chicana and had witnessed certain rites that she was an expert. She studied them and was trained by teachers. Not wanting to engage in the irresponsible use of ancient traditional knowledge, she made sure to learn as much as possible before practicing as a curandera. She is not herself an ancient Mayan or Mexica, but her people are related to these people, so she made a point of studying them in order to practice in an authentic and ethical way.

Being authentic does not mean you can only practice the traditions of your known ancestors or only practice those traditions you grew up practicing. Such limitations would ignore the effects of slavery, colonialism, and various postcolonial practices designed to separate colonized people from their traditions. Many BIPOC people were not allowed to pass down their traditions; they had their culture outlawed or were severely punished, imprisoned, or killed for practicing it. Being authentic does not mean you have to have verifiable blood ties to the traditions. Biological essentialism, besides being based on an unscientific belief in races, also does not take into account the existence of numerous healers like myself who are mixed blood, born into more than one culture.

African Americans, denied access to knowledge of their ancestral cultural practices, have had to travel to Africa and the Caribbean to reacquaint themselves with traditions they suspect, but can never know for sure, were practiced by their ancestors. Similarly, Native Americans, after conquest, removal, termination, and reorganization, have often been cut off from traditional cultural practices and have developed pan-Indian traditions. Urban Indians have cultural practices that may not always correspond with their exact tribal heritage because 1) they may be a mixture of tribes; 2) due to adoption, they may not know their tribe; or 3) they may more authentically identify with a pan-Indian community they grew up in than with a tribal or reservation community.

Transracially adopted persons from Asian, African, and Native American cultures may have to acquaint themselves with their traditions or traditions like theirs as adults. This reacquainting is not the same as cultural appropriation. What is problematic is when people decide to study the traditions of other people despite having no ties to the tradition and then go on to set themselves up as experts on that culture and become spokespersons and even gatekeepers of it. If they use what they have learned to become experts and then use that expertise to dominate or control that field for power or financial gain, they are culturally appropriating, and that is unethical.

You do not have to be white or of European ancestry to engage in cultural appropriation, but it happens most often in these communities because of the histories of colonialism and the current structures of racist patriarchy and global North/South inequalities. When a Westerner or a white person begins practicing the traditions of the peoples they have oppressed, colonized, conquered, or enslaved, there are often problems of cultural appropriation. The relationship between oppressor and oppressed, first world/third world or North/South is an unequal power relationship. Whenever a person or culture with unearned privilege begins to practice the culture of the people they have power and privilege over, the unequal power dynamic affects how that choice is received. The privileged persons are often automatically given a higher platform from which to practice or teach the cultural traditions they have adopted. The privileged person who studies with an Indian guru in India comes back to the US and quickly rises to the status of guru by virtue of the tendency of white people to prefer to learn about spiritual traditions from other white people. The resources and status that whites have access to allows them to turn what they have learned into courses, workshops, and positions of power. One of the negative effects of this cultural appropriation is that such people replace the actual authentic teachers with themselves. Instead of encouraging other white people to go to India and study with the guru, they offer teachings for a substantially higher fee at home.

I once knew a white American who was regularly traveling to Peru to engage in Ayahuasca ceremonies with a medicine man. He liked it so much he kept going back. He then began buying up crafts from the village and taking them back to the United States to sell. He marked up these craft items 500 percent because of the low standard of living in the village and the poor exchange rate. Next, he began bringing the medicine man up to the United States, holding ceremonies in the US for money, and keeping part of the proceeds for himself. Finally, he decided to start holding his own ceremonies in the US without bothering with the expense of bringing the medicine man up. He claimed he had been trained by the medicine man and could now hold his own ceremonies. Americans who might have normally traveled to Peru to do ceremony with the medicine man were now giving their money to this white man who had worked with the medicine man for a short period of time.

The unequal power dynamic between the American and the medicine man made it difficult for the medicine man to discipline the young white disciple. His village needed the monies they gained from the sale of their crafts. The money he received from the trips also went toward feeding the whole village. Even though the young white disciple was keeping 80 percent of the proceeds from his sales of their crafts and 50 percent of the fees for the ceremonies, the money the villagers did receive made a difference in their impoverished lives. They were in no position to negotiate for a fairer share. The medicine man was in no position to demand certain disciplines from the disciple.

The unequal power dynamic that was the result of the relationship between Peru and the United States, as well as the historic relationship between Indios and blancos in the Americas, had an overdetermining impact on their interaction and led to an unethical interpersonal dynamic.

The white American man set himself up as an expert on a culture he had visited and began to make a serious profit off of what he had learned. His cultural appropriation allowed him to make a living off of somebody else's culture, and he stopped deferring to the wisdom of the actual culture-bearer because his privilege allowed him to do so.

CULTURAL APPROPRIATION QUESTIONS TO ASK YOURSELF

1. Do you actually have the authority to practice the tradition, and if so, who or what gave you that authority?

2. How did the tradition reach you? Study and research your traditions. Make a point of knowing where they came from. Who are your teachers? Who taught them?

3. Do you satisfy the requirements for becoming a teacher in that tradition *according to that tradition* (for example in some traditions you have to be called by a dream or spirit sickness to become a shaman; in others you have to be chosen by a medicine person)?

4. Is your practice respectful of the *actual people* who created the tradition? (For example, do you like sweat lodges but disrespect Natives? Do you love Rootwork but disrespect Blacks? Do you only like the ancient versions of the people who originated this tradition?)

5. Are you contributing to the community that birthed the tradition you practice? (For example, have you taken the

practices out of the original community in order to teach them exclusively to your community or to white people? And if so, how is that benefitting the original community?)

6. Have you set yourself up as an authority over someone else's tradition, thus displacing authentic culture-bearers? (Are you paid to headline conferences talking about the tradition while actual members of those communities are absent from the podium? Is your book considered the standard source on the tradition while the books of actual culture-bearers are not even available in bookstores?)

TRAIT #3: BEING SELF-AWARE

Being *self-aware* is knowing one's strengths and weaknesses, one's wounds and vulnerabilities, and one's needs and desires. This quality is essential to being an ethical psychic. When you hang a shingle as a psychic, people will come to you asking you to do all kinds of things. It is important to know what you can and cannot do so that you do not make promises you cannot keep or endeavor to do things you lack the skills to do. Over-committing and over-promising can prove disastrous and harmful. For example, if a client asks for information that requires predicting the future (e.g., Will this investment pay off? Will I get the job? Will I recover from this illness?), you should not attempt to provide that information if you have never demonstrated a gift for precognition. Instead, inform your client that seeing the future is not one of your gifts.

We are not all born with the same gifts. Some psychics are talented telepaths as well, but most are not. Some psychics, like the famous Uri Geller, are able to move objects with their minds, but most are not. We may also be limited in our gifts because of our lack of training and experience. If you are an excellent intuitive, but you have no experience identifying physical disease in the body, you should not call yourself a medical intuitive. If you are an excellent medium but you have no experience solving crimes with your gifts, you should not claim to be a psychic detective.

Another source of limitation can be emotional proclivities or wounds. If, for example, you have suffered a large number of losses this year, working with the grieving may not be the best idea. You may be unable to perform at your usual level because the subject is too close to home. Have you recently extricated yourself from a messy and painful divorce? If so, you may not be the best psychic to provide relationship coaching. Are you currently suffering from a painful condition? If so, work that involves tuning into other peoples' physical pains may not be a good choice at this time. Sometimes you will have to cancel a client or take a break from providing certain services because you are self-aware enough to know that you will not be able to do your best under the current conditions or given your current limitations. The following are important edicts for self-awareness:

1. If you are aware that you are under great emotional strain, avoid working clairsentiently. Turn off your clairsentience or take a break from doing psychic work.

2. If you are aware that you are afraid of ghosts, evil spirits, or spirits overpowering you, do not do spirit release work.

3. If you are aware that you are sexually attracted to your client, refrain from engaging in energy healing work on them to avoid sending sexual energy to them during the healing session.

4. If you come from a family of alcoholics or addicts and you tend to develop codependent traits when working with addicts, choose not to work with that population or delay working with them until you have addressed your own codependency issues.

5. If you are aware that you are still grieving the loss of a loved one, decide not to do mediumship work for a while.

6. If you are aware that you have strong beliefs or judgements about certain groups (religions, careers, etc.) based on upbringing or previous bad experiences, avoid working with those groups until you have processed your own feelings about those groups.

TRAIT #4: LEARNING FROM MISTAKES AND BEING HUMBLE

In order to be an ethical psychic, you must be able to receive feedback, accept criticism, acknowledge mistakes, and continue to grow. The very best psychics in the world are still only 80 to 90 percent accurate. Chances are, if you have not become famous or wildly successful as a direct result of your skills, your accuracy rate is lower. You may be accurate about 70 percent of the time. This means you are wrong 30 percent of the time. With practice, most psychics can improve their accuracy rates, but the key to gaining a greater proficiency over time is knowing when you are making mistakes.

It is not possible to learn from mistakes unless we acknowledge we are making them. The best source for knowledge about our mistakes is our clients. Making a point of getting feedback from our clients on a regular basis is essential to improving our craft. And the better we are at providing accurate readings and guidance, the more likely we are to help and not harm our clients.

Because clients often take what we say seriously, being as accurate as possible is often equivalent to being as helpful as possible. A reading that is 70 percent accurate can be very persuasive. If 70 percent of what you say is spot on, then the client may tend to believe the 30 percent that is inaccurate as well. And this could be detrimental. If you give the client the impression that you are 100 percent accurate and they believe you and they take action based on a piece of information you gave them, which was inaccurate, this can create problems in their life. What if, for example, you describe the personality traits, strengths, and weaknesses of their partner and the problems in their relationship with 100 percent accuracy— but then you tell them their partner is having an affair. If it turns out you are inaccurate about the affair because you are tuning into their suspicions or you are tuning into their partner's fantasies rather than their actions, this could be a problem. The client, if of a highly jealous temperament, may leave, malign, or harm his partner, cheat her in a divorce proceeding, or abandon his child because he feels betrayed. Because of your accuracy during most of the reading, the client believes *all* of the reading. It is our responsibility to know this and to guard against it.

As noted, accuracy has ethical ramifications. Being inaccurate about certain topics can result in extreme consequences. We cannot expect to be 100 percent accurate, but we can dedicate ourselves to becoming as accurate as possible and we can remain humble, knowing that we are bound to make mistakes. The best way to do this is through practice, by seeking ongoing training, learning from our mistakes, and admitting to clients that we are not always 100 percent accurate.

The importance of practice cannot be overstated. Too many psychics hang a shingle before they are truly ready and, as a result, offer inconsistent readings. When you are not competent and confident, you will be tempted to engage in unethical behaviors, telling clients what they want to hear or glossing over your mistakes. Psychic/Shaman Freya Rey explains, "Learning to be a psychic requires an intense commitment of time and energy. You should be prepared to invest years of effort and hundreds of free readings to bring your skills to a professional level."[13]

Learning from Your Mistakes

Sometimes clients deny the truth because they lack self-awareness, but sometimes they deny the reading because you have told them something inaccurate. The psychic seeking to learn from her mistakes will dedicate herself to learning to discern the difference between these two nos. If a client insists that you are wrong about something, apologize and inform them that you are never 100 percent accurate and that you value the feedback. If you have told the client something inaccurate, listen to their feedback about how what you said was wrong.

When giving hugely impactful information, tread carefully and inform the client that you could be wrong. For example, if you see a deadly disease, you can say to the client, "I am picking up on a very serious disease that requires immediate medical attention. I may be wrong, and I hope that I am, but this is what I am getting."

If you are getting something wrong, try to determine why you are getting it wrong—whether it is a misinterpretation of true information, an unclear symbol, or something else. Look for patterns in your mistakes. What type of information tends to be difficult for you to get accurately? Reflect and ask yourself if there is a reason you get certain types of information wrong. For example, are you often wrong when you work on relationship issues? Cause of death issues? Predictions? Is there something in your own life or in your own training that could explain these mistakes? Taking the time to reflect on these questions will help you become an ethical psychic.

Be Humble

The importance of being humble cannot be emphasized enough. When a psychic becomes arrogant, they are prone to making mistakes and less likely to learn from these mistakes. They are also less likely to be compassionate to the needs of their client and less likely to be aware of their own limitations. Psychic talents are not earned, they are bestowed, and this is why we call them gifts. Nobody ought to brag about having psychic gifts any more than someone born beautiful should brag about their beauty. We can work hard to develop and perfect our gifts and can rightly be proud of any efforts we have put into developing a disciplined control of our gifts, but it is important to remember—they are gifts.

Sometimes students ask me how they can be confident and also be humble. As a psychic develops, it is important that they acquire the necessary confidence to be secure enough to give readings. Doubt and self-censorship are obstacles that beginning psychics must overcome. So how does one become confident without becoming overly confident? First, it is essential to understand that confidence is a prerequisite for being humble. It is only when you know that you are great that you can make a concentrated effort to downplay your greatness. It is only when others are consistently praising you that it becomes important not to get lost in that. If you are full of self-doubt and lacking in self-confidence, your refusal to sing your own praises or accept praise from others is not humility, it is low self-esteem.

Humbleness entails knowing your greatness and yet knowing how much more you have to learn. A wise person, Socrates once said, is a person who understands that the more he learns the more he recognizes he does not know. In explaining the wisdom to be found in humility, Socrates once explained his own wisdom in this way: "Although [some] people know nothing they all believe they know something; whereas I, if I know nothing, at least have no doubts about it."[14] Despite his wisdom, he never came to believe that he was wise or that he knew all there was to know. He always maintained an awareness of his ignorance and urged others to do the same. It was this humility that actually made him wise. A humble person is a perpetual student. She knows that there is more to learn, and she assumes there are many others out in the world who know more than she does. By remaining humble, despite having acquired clear proficiency, psychics keep themselves open to learning more and to expanding their gifts. If, no matter how many modality certificates you earn and how many positive reviews you receive, you recognize that there is always more to learn, you recognize there are limits to what you know, and you remain aware of the fact that you can still make mistakes, you will become a humble and ethical psychic.

The most effective means for recognizing a good psychic is by looking at the effects of her work. If her gift is accurate and reliable, that is very good. But if the use of said gifts doesn't yield positive demonstrable outcomes, the gift is probably not helping anyone. The ethical psychic seeks to help and never harm in the employ of her gifts. Pay attention to the effect that you have on your clients to ensure your gifts are truly beneficial. Do not just rest on your laurels after you have achieved a certain level of accomplishment or have received a certain level of praise. Pay attention to the results of your work. Sometimes what worked last year will not work this year, or what worked on one client will not work on the next. Ethical, humble psychics pay attention to what actually results from their practice and do not satisfy themselves with just having good intentions. Looking at the results is not the same as listening to feedback. Sometimes a client does not give the psychic credit, but their life improves, and their problems go away. Regardless of whether or not the client thanks you or praises you, look at the effects of your work. Is the client better off after seeing you?

Arrogant psychics are dangerous. They are so convinced of their infallibility that they easily overlook mistakes and disregard criticism from others. As a result, they are unable to avoid harming their clients and are also unavailable to repair the damage that they inflict. Becoming impervious to critique inhibits a psychic's growth. Becoming impervious to praise is the goal of the ethical psychic.

EXAMPLES OF BEING HUMBLE

1. If a client tells you that another well-respected psychic gave a radically different answer to their question, consider the possibility that you could be wrong and the other psychic could be right.

2. Do not brag about your abilities or your accuracy rate. If you are really that good, others will brag for you. Direct potential clients to satisfied clients who can describe how you helped them.

3. Accept criticism graciously. Avoid becoming defensive. Consider all criticism as an opportunity to learn and grow.

4. Look for psychics and healers who know more than you/are more successful than you—and consult.

5. Keep learning. Take classes. Attend workshops. Read books. Identify your weaknesses and pursue the practices needed to change weaknesses into strengths.

TRAIT #5: BEING SENSITIVE TO CLIENT NEEDS

The ethical psychic is compassionate and sensitive to the needs of their clients. They don't only listen to Spirit or only act in accordance with their training. They are also aware of what the client needs and wants. Not every client wants to heal and grow at the rate you think they should. Not every client wants the unvarnished truth. Not every client wants to know their diagnosis, and addicts often do not want to become sober. Psychics and healers must resist the temptation to save their clients. They must resist the call of the ego that tells them that they always know what is best for their client.

If your client is not happy with the service you are providing, pay attention to what they are saying so that you can learn and improve. If, for example, you like to "just tell it like you get it," but your brusque manner causes many of your clients to cry and to become overcome with grief and so distressed that they are unable to use the information to improve their lives, you may want to reconsider your communication style. If you are providing a certain type of information but the clients are coming to you asking for a different type of information, you may need to reevaluate your work. It is not okay just to say that "Spirit wants me to work this way" and then work that way regardless of how it is received by humans. Ask for feedback on a regular basis and take it seriously.

If your primary purpose as a psychic is to be of service, then it is important to know exactly what service potential clients want and need. Tuning into the client and using your clairsentience to determine what your clients need is essential to being of service to them. It is important to listen to what clients say and also tune in to what they feel.

Being aware of what your clients' wants and needs are is just the first step in being compassionate. We must also address their needs in a nonjudgmental way, to the extent morally possible. As psychics we should never feel we must encourage harmful acts or contribute to the actions of others that we find morally reprehensible. However, we should be careful not to allow ego, in the form of judgments, to prevent us from healing clients in the way that they need to be helped. If we are more concerned with making our own judgments about what we think they need, we may do more harm than good.

Spirit does not judge. So, when we find ourselves making decisions about how to assist clients and find that our decisions are heavily influenced by our own personal judgments of them, we should stop and reevaluate. Judging your clients is rarely helpful and it will get in the way of your ability to get pure information about them. Striking a balance between avoiding irrelevant judgments and having a clear sense of moral boundaries is key. For example, if a client asks for information about the two relationships she is in, and you have a strong belief in monogamy, you may be tempted to judge her choices, and this may interfere with your ability to get accurate and useful information. Your preferences, assumptions, beliefs, stereotypes, and prejudices are manifestations of the ego and its need to be right. Relying on these beliefs and prejudices in a reading increases the chances of you providing faulty or harmful information because of the filter of bias through which you are receiving and interpreting information.

Issues of privacy must also be taken into account when you are answering questions about persons other than your client. If a client comes to you asking for information about, for example, their lover's husband, you may want to refuse to provide this information on the grounds that it would be an invasion of the husband's privacy. Similarly, if one of the people your client is asking about was merely a crush, then you will be limited in the amount of information you can provide without invading the privacy of the "crush."

In the earlier example in which the client was asking about information related to her two partners, because she was in a relationship with both people, she had energetic cords with both of them and access to information about both. However, in the second example, the client had no relationship and no energetic cords with the husband of their lover and thus no right to that information. Thus, regardless of your personal beliefs about polyamorous versus monogamous relationships, you can give the first client information about both these lovers because she is already connected to them in mutually consenting relationships. Considering the privacy of the people you are tuning into is your responsibility as a psychic. Advising or judging clients with regard to the types of relationships they enter into is not your responsibility or your job.

As a psychic, keep your focus and attention on the needs of the client. This will make it easier to avoid letting your ego get in the way. Asking clients what they need and using your gifts of clairsentience to tune in to what they need and what they are feeling can be far more useful in helping you to decide what information to deliver than focusing on your own beliefs, assumptions, and judgments.

It is important to always take into account your clients' feelings. Did you just bring through a deceased family member who is cold and uncaring and speaks in that way? Should you deliver what the selfish spirit has to say, despite the fact that the client is distraught and crying? Perhaps not. If you tune in and feel how that message will negatively impact the client, you may choose not to deliver that message or delay its delivery. Have you discovered that your client's marriage is going to end in divorce? Is your client's child going to die? Is your client making poor business choices that could result in the loss of their business? Think about how you will deliver this message before delivering it. Ask Spirit, tune in to your client, and then think through what is the best way to give out the information you get. Contrary to what some psychics believe, psychic work is not inimical to the rational or logical mind. Intuition and rationality must be combined to provide the best reading.

EXAMPLES OF BEING SENSITIVE

1. If a client comes to you asking for relationship help, do not assume they want you to give them medical information just because that is what you picked up.

2. If a client comes to you asking for help with overcoming addiction, do not assume it's appropriate to do spirit release work on them unless you talk to them first.

3. If a client is in a relationship with someone who is not a good match for them, but they have come to you asking for advice on how to save the marriage/partnership, give them that advice rather than telling them it is hopeless. They may need to try everything before they are willing to walk away. Instead, ask to receive information that will assist the client on their own chosen path.

4. If someone comes to you asking for the physical cause of an illness or symptom, do not give them the emotional cause.

5. Give people what they think *they* need before giving them what *you* think they need. After they have gotten their most pressing questions answered, it is possible they might be open to addressing other issues.

As you can see, being an ethical psychic is not as straightforward as it might seem. Part of the task of the ethical psychic is getting out of the way. How do we set aside the moral beliefs that cause us to judge others while still maintaining the moral compass necessary to be a good psychic? I have found that being humble and listening to a higher source has been key to helping me discern how to do the right thing versus doing what I think is right.

TRAIT #6: LISTENING TO A HIGHER SOURCE

The most helpful psychics get assistance from a higher source. When you get your information from a higher source than yourself or your client, you are less likely to give messages that can harm your client because you are not as heavily conditioned by the needs of the ego. You are also likely to get information of a higher vibration.

South African/Tswana Sangoma (medicine man) Isaac Mayeng cautions against being the type of healer who does not listen to a higher source. Some self-taught healers, he writes,

are more like technicians. They have no common code of conduct. There is no "contact" between them and a higher power, to heal and never harm. There is not a strong and binding belief that they are simply the messengers or the pipeline, the instruments of the ancestors and God. Some of this group are only interested in the practice . . . for the money it can bring them.[15]

Some psychics tune in to the aura of their clients to get information. Some psychics use telepathy. Some use spirit guides or ancestors to receive information, while others use remote viewing. Eventually a developing psychic should come to rely on high vibration sources of information. High vibration sources include your Higher Self, angels, archangels, ascended masters, spiritual teachers, healing ancestors, and God/Source/Creator, among others. The higher your source, the purer the information. A higher source will never lead you astray, make you feel bad, or retard your soul growth in any way.

Humans, on the other hand, whether dead or alive, can easily lead a client astray. If you are getting information from guides who are spirits/deceased humans/ancestors, and you have not been trained in an ancestor religion or healing tradition, there is no guarantee that the information you receive will be of the highest and best. Dead people are only capable of giving information from their own level of consciousness and soul growth. Recognizing the limits of sources that are not highly evolved souls is important for the ethical psychic seeking to do no harm. Grandpa Joe may have been a wise elder when he was alive, but if Grandpa hasn't evolved since leaving the Earth plane, his information will not necessarily be coming from a higher source than Earth. If he is more highly evolved than you, then he is a good choice, but you may need to go beyond Grandpa for certain information.

There is an exception to be noted: if you are trained in a traditional form of healing like Sangoma, which relies on ancestors to assist with healing, you are indeed dealing with a higher level of spirit. These ancestors are spirit doctors, or guides who had some type of healing gift or training when they were alive, and they are able to guide healers from a higher vibration on the Other Side. The danger comes when people who have received no such training just decide to indiscriminately contact their ancestors. In Southern African traditional healing practices like that found in Sangoma, the ancestors choose the healer, not the other way around. A healer has a calling and then the ancestors assist them. According to medicine man Dr. Nhlavana Maseko, founder of the Traditional Healers Organization (THO) of Africa, "Possessed healers, healers with a spiritual calling from the ancestors cannot harm their patients or others by virtue of their calling."[16]

Numerous traditions exist that train people how to safely connect with high level ancestors. Santeria in Cuba, Shango in Trinidad, Candomblé in Brazil, Taoism in China, and many shamanistic traditions worldwide involve working with ancestors. Indiscriminately calling down ancestors is not the same as working within one of these spiritual traditions.

There exist numerous magickal traditions in which people seek to bind or control spirits or ancestors for their own purposes. You can find many books that introduce beginners to the art of summoning spirits. (In these traditions where summoning spirits is considered a normal part of the craft, spirits are not perceived as having rights, and forcing them to work for you is considered acceptable behavior.) Such practitioners will bind *jinn*, astral beings, *egregore, servitors*, interdimensional beings, or demons to obtain power, money, or other desirables.[17] True wiccans will tell you that summoning is a skill that takes years of study to learn how to do safely. [18]

When you seek to control spirits, not only do you put yourself at risk of possession, but there is no guarantee that the information you receive will provide insight from a higher source. Just because you can get a spirit to work for you doesn't mean the spirit will always tell you the truth. Eventually, spirits tend to break free of the chains that bind them and they often take retribution. When you deal with such spirits, there is no guarantee you will get enlightened information and once you work in this way, there is a chance you will never be able to tell who you are dealing with in the future. Inexperienced psychics are often tempted to work with spirit slaves in order to acquire things. Because you do not need to raise your vibration or live in a good way to call such spirits, working with them is easier than working with high-level spirits. But there is a price for everything. When you do this work without the protection of a Higher Power, you are at risk for not only getting bad information but also for getting harmed.

Keep in mind also that both deceased relatives and "spirits for hire" tend to have self-interested reasons for providing the information that they do. For example, if Periamma wants you to marry a nice Indian boy, she may give you information that will push you in that direction even if that does not align with your soul growth. If Great-Grandpa Yokchee wants you to preserve the cultural traditions passed down through the generations, he may direct you away from learning other traditions that could help you to be an even better healer than he was.

African American medium, Peter Brown, explains the importance of working with a Higher Power in mediumship:

> *Disembodied intelligences call what I do "Inspirational Writing" as opposed to "automatic writing" . . . there is a distinct difference. In automatic writing, you pick up a pen and wait. You take whatever you get. That is not necessarily good because there are intelligences that will play with you . . . with inspirational writing, you begin each session with a prayer. You ask for divine guidance. Then you have specific questions which you present. And these are answered."[19]*

When a psychic does not work with a Higher Power, they open themselves up to the influence of lower-level spirits and astral beings. What Peter is referring to is the way in which all kinds of spurious information can come through during a mediumship session or automatic writing session, or while a psychic is using any other tool to perform a reading or healing where they haven't made any effort to filter the guidance. He calls it *automatic writing* when a low-level spirit comes through and *Inspirational Writing* when a high-level spirit comes. When psychics can recognize higher- versus lower-level spirits and set the intention (through prayer or ritual, for example) to only work with higher-level beings, they protect themselves from the malign influences of such spirits. Psychics whose only interest is making money or acquiring fame will sometimes work with low-level spirits, earthbound spirits, jinns, or demons, even though they know working with such beings will likely result in someone being hurt. Other psychics are simply ignorant of the dangers of unwittingly working with such entities. An ethical psychic takes every precaution to make sure they do not expose themselves or their clients to nefarious spirits. An ethical psychic should have a connection to a very high source such as Spirit, Higher Self, Universe, God, Creator, The Great I Am, or similar entities. Setting the intention to work with a Higher Power protects the psychic, allows the psychic to receive reliable guidance, and ensures that the information the psychic is receiving is "for the highest and best."

Regardless of whether or not a psychic is religious, believing in a Higher Power protects them and also helps them avoid the tyranny of the ego. When a psychic has a connection to a Higher Power, they are able to connect to this source and obtain information untainted by their own cognitive or emotive limitations.

LISTENING TO A HIGHER SOURCE

1. A psychic who knows her gift comes from a higher source will never take credit for all her successes in the use of said gift.

2. A psychic who has a relationship with a higher source can receive high-vibration guidance, thus making her a better psychic-healer.

3. A psychic with a connection to Source will have a check on the ego.

4. A psychic with a connection to a higher source will be aligned with high-vibration energy and thus will be better equipped to help people operating from a lower vibrational field.

5. A psychic with a connection to her Higher Self has access to unlimited wisdom and as a result will not be tempted to involve herself with modalities or approaches that appeal to fear, insecurity, and a desire for power.

An aspiring psychic who takes the time to cultivate the traits discussed will not have to worry about harming anyone with their gifts. They won't have to learn the hard way what not to do. Cultivating these traits can save the developing psychic from a lot of heartache. A psychic who is motivated by service rather than money or status is much less likely to take advantage of vulnerable clients either wittingly or unwittingly. A self-aware psychic who is true to themselves and practices with authenticity will not have to worry about what the latest fads are and will not have to pretend to have skills they do not have. They will not have to undo any damage caused by trying to be someone they are not. A psychic who is sensitive to a client's needs won't have to deal with excessive complaints from clients. The psychic who is humble will learn from their mistakes rather than seek to always be right. And finally, a practitioner who is guided by some spirit or being larger than themselves will not have to worry about being led astray by dark forces that can then misinform or hurt their clients.

2

THE RISKS OF PSYCHIC WORK

Mediumship is not entertainment. It's not about ego. It's not something you do to get rich. But mediums do have to earn a living. It does not involve playing on the grieving or making people dependent on what you have to tell them. It is not about power . . . It's about humility.[1]

—JANET NOHAVEC, *WHERE TWO WORLDS MEET*

Psychics have powers that non-psychics do not. They possess knowledge and gifts that give them an advantage over others. This creates a power dynamic between psychics and non-psychics, and often between psychics and their clients. Whenever there is a power dynamic, there is a risk that power will be abused. For this reason, psychic work is prone to abuses of power. In addition, people who seek the services of psychics (even if they are themselves psychics) are often in distress and in need of guidance or assistance to help them solve problems and make important life choices. For this reason, they are more vulnerable and more susceptible to suggestions than usual.

The fact that psychics have privileged access to knowledge that average humans do not have gives their messages an added authority. It is important that psychics do not take advantage of the susceptibility of their clients and it is important that they are cognizant of the way their words may be perceived. A psychic cannot be casual or cavalier in her delivery of information. She cannot simply claim her gifts are for entertainment purposes only and go on her merry way. Psychics must strive to be ethical in their dealings with clients, for the risks of becoming unethical are many. As psychic Alexandra Chauran explains,

> *Psychics have incredible power . . . the power to influence other people's behavior in a deep and meaningful way. Psychics are the spiritual leaders of a generation and comprise a culture of people who value intuition. Whether a psychic accepts this responsibility or not, it is received and sometimes recklessly abused.*[2]

By being aware of the many risks that attend psychic work, the psychic can quite consciously seek to avoid misusing their power. So many risks exist, including invading people's privacy, creating client dependency, exploiting clients financially, and making matters worse, among others. Once the practicing psychic, healer, or medicine person is aware of these risks and how they manifest, they are easy to avoid.

UNETHICAL RISK #1:
INVADING THE PRIVACY OF OTHERS

The most obvious risk entailed in working as a psychic is accidentally invading the privacy of another. Supersensory individuals have information that most people do not have. This means they have access to information about people that these people have not openly shared. A psychic can easily become a snoop or a spy, peering into the personal lives of others at will. In order to avoid this invasion, the psychic must make the privacy of others a priority. Psychics who do not think about privacy issues or take steps to guard against transgressions will invariably trample on the privacy rights of others. This is an abuse of their gifts and it is unethical.

When I was a child, I developed a classification system for psychics. It was simplistic but it will serve our purposes here. I distinguish between two types of psychics: *mind-pickers* and *mind-knowers*. A *mind-picker* is someone who reaches out without consent and "picks" information from a person. They read minds, read auras, reach out, and get as much information as they can scan about a person—all without asking. A *mind-knower*, on the other hand, is a supersensory person, who, without trying, spontaneously knows things about people and chooses to be disciplined about this knowledge. When a psychic is conducting a reading, she is reaching out and reading her client but only because they asked her to and they are paying her to do so. I decided at age eight that I would be a mind-knower and never a mind-picker. In other words, without having the adult language to articulate what I believed, I decided as a baby psychic that it was not right to invade the privacy of others. And while I have developed other beliefs as I have grown up, I continue to believe that mind-picking is wrong.

Beyond these fundamental commitments, the psychic still faces the risk of accidentally invading another's privacy. There was a time in my life when I was developing my gifts, attending classes, honing my skills, and getting bombarded with information. Perhaps because I was finally saying an unequivocal yes to my gifts and studying (I had maintained an ambivalence to my super senses for much of my life), my gifts were expanding at an accelerated rate. During this period, every time someone shook my hand or hugged me, I got information about their physical and/or mental health. I was not seeking out this information; it came to me unbidden. Nevertheless, I felt certain that most if not all of the time, these people would not be happy to know that I knew these things about them.

When you are the spontaneous recipient of information about another, you have access to private matters without intending to. However, a psychic can invade the privacy of others in less-innocent circumstances. One such circumstance involves answering questions that the clients ask about other people. Oftentimes, clients will ask me questions about their loved ones, bosses, colleagues, neighbors, and exes. Because they have energetic cords linking them to most of these people, I often determine that they have the right to access information about these people as long as the information relates specifically to the client. But sometimes people want to know things that they really have no right to know, and in order to answer their questions, I would have to violate the privacy of someone else. Any time a psychic sits down with a client to discuss "relationships" she risks violating someone's privacy, and the ethical psychic must consider this carefully.

Another instance in which a psychic risks invading privacy is when a client asks me to do a scan or reading for someone else. For example, in my practice as a medical intuitive, I often get requests from family members and spouses to do medical scans on people who know nothing about the scan. If I were to consent to do such a scan, I would be providing private health information to the friends and relatives of someone without their consent. To avoid this, I do not do third-party scans. When I do a scan, I require the consent of the patient regardless of who is paying.

Another type of service ripe for creating problems with privacy is reading the Akashic Records. The *Akashic Records* is an energetic library that holds the records of your soul's path in its various incarnations. We all have access to our own Akashic Records, but supersensory persons with a certain level of gift can access the records of others. A psychic with this gift may be tempted to access the records of another person without that person's permission if they are in a close relationship with that person. Similarly, a client may want a psychic to open the records of a loved one without proper consent. Doing so would be unethical. Individual Akashic Records belong to individual souls. Rifling through them without permission is akin to rifling through someone's desk without permission. An ethical psychic never consents to do such work for her client.

In addition to professional risks, casual privacy invasions must be avoided at all cost. Sometimes, as psychics are developing their gifts, they run around reading everyone they meet. In the same way that a child who learns to do a cartwheel will often do cartwheels anywhere and everywhere, undisciplined psychics will sometimes be so eager to practice or show off their gift that they will not consider the effects of their actions. You may find yourself tempted to tune in to a friend or coworker who is asking for your advice. But if the friend did not ask you for a reading and is only asking you for your advice, it is not appropriate to start reading them in the context of a casual conversation. Likewise, just because you spontaneously get information about a colleague or stranger does not mean you should share it with them. This can be perceived as you nosing around in their private affairs, which is not ethical.

UNETHICAL RISK #2: CLIENT DEPENDENCY

Most people consult psychics because they are in need. Although some people consult psychics for fun or entertainment purposes, most clients who seek the advice of psychics are looking for answers to important questions and they visit a psychic-healer to address something bigger than a minor transitory condition. Increasingly, people consult psychics in a life-coaching role. When a client employs the services of a coach or healer on a regular basis, they run the risk of becoming emotionally dependent upon the psychic.

The ethical psychic does whatever she can to avoid her clients becoming emotionally dependent upon her. An emotionally dependent client will find it difficult to make decisions on their own. They will feel they have to consult their psychic often and will feel unable to take action without her input. This is unhealthy and will result in impairments for the client. It also sets up conditions in which abuse is more likely to occur. In addition to crippling the client's ability to make their own decisions, an emotional dependency can also adversely affect the client's relationships with others and can lead them to believe that the psychic is the sole authority for their life. They may give their power away and be unable to engage in healthy relationships with others.

Psychic and author Alexandra Chauran explains that setting expectations before the reading is very important for clients. By letting clients know what you can and cannot do, you address unrealistic client expectations. Let the client know the limits of what you can do and that you cannot solve all of their problems, nor should you try.[3] Reiki practitioner Penelope Quest, in her book, *Reiki for Life*, explains the importance of setting boundaries with clients. It is "unacceptable to exploit your clients either financially or emotionally by insisting on regular appointments or by making them feel dependent upon you."[4] The ethical psychic believes in client empowerment and honors the trust clients have given them.

Emotional dependence is not healthy for the psychic or the client. But a psychic with an unhealthy emotional need for praise or control may encourage dependency in their clients. Emotional dependency can also be quite profitable. Unethical psychics can count on emotionally dependent clients to pay their car notes and rent each month. Some psychics use their gifts to coerce clients into returning again and again, even when the client isn't experiencing improvement or growth. The client's stagnancy guarantees the psychic a consistent income. If the client becomes "healthy," independent, or whole again, they no longer need the psychic. The ethical psychic, whose primary motivation is service, never sacrifices the client's well-being for money, esteem, or control.

Healthy relationships are characterized by reciprocity. The psychic-client relationship is an exchange of services for money or something of value; it is a financial relationship and therefore developing intense emotional bonds with the client is simply not appropriate. Because of the unique vulnerabilities inherent in the psychic-client relationship, the risk of developing emotional bonds is great. The psychic may provide information of an intimate nature. She may know things about the client that nobody else does. The client often tells the psychic her secrets. Because some people are unwilling or even averse to working with therapists, they may come to psychics for counseling or coaching to address their most intense emotional issues. The intimacy and vulnerability that the client feels with the psychic can evolve into dependency; the ethical psychic must be aware of this risk and take precautions to prevent it.

If a psychic is actually helping the client, then over time the client should need the psychic less and less, or else they should be resolving problems in certain areas and moving on to other areas. If, for example, a client comes to you for help with a relationship, the help you provide should improve that relationship. In subsequent sessions the client should be coming to discuss other relationships or other issues in their life. In other words, the client should be making progress. The client should not be coming to you again and again with the same questions and showing no perceptible growth.

Canadian Psychic Colette Baron-Reid identifies the psychic's ability to resist client dependency as one of the traits of a reputable psychic. She explains:

> *A reputable psychic will never create a dependency. You should never feel like you need a psychic to always show you what's next. We are all spiritual beings with different levels of intuition, and you should feel comfortable listening to your own intuition with assistance of a reading, not a dependency on it. If you do want help with what action steps will lead you to your desired path, seek out the support of an intuitive coach.*[5]

I had a client once who came to me about problems she was having with her husband. I warned her about his mental illness and his plan to sue for custody of their child if she divorced him. I told her he was meeting with lawyers and was plotting with other family members. She only listened to half of the advice I gave her. While following my advice helped her, the warnings that she failed to heed and the protective measures that she failed to take caused her to always be in distress. Instead of taking steps to protect herself (like providing the documentation to her lawyer to pursue the case), she would simply wait for the next crisis and then call me. Over time I realized she had developed an emotional dependency on me. She refused to consult a therapist, despite my recommendation that she do so; I had unwittingly become her crisis hotline. However, having a crisis hotline was not what she needed. She needed to take concrete steps to improve her situation. When I realized she was becoming emotionally dependent upon my readings, I stopped seeing her. Although it could be argued that my readings were helping her, I also worried that they were hurting her. She was not reaching out to the people she needed help from. Maybe, I thought, if she no longer had me to depend upon, she would start to reach out to friends, therapists, family members, and lawyers.

The primary motivation of an ethical psychic is service. But being of service is not enough. An ethical psychic must ensure that the service they provided does not come at the price of emotional dependency. Signs of emotional dependency include these:

1. The client is unable to make any important decisions without first consulting their psychic.

2. Whenever the client is in crisis, they call their psychic before or in lieu of calling friends, family, partners, or therapists.

3. The client has to see the psychic frequently and increases their visits to the psychic over time.

4. When the client encounters friends and family members who disagree with their psychic, they disregard the advice these people give in favor of following the psychic's advice, regardless of the fallout that may ensue from such a decision.

5. The client has the psychic on speed-dial or calls or texts them frequently after business hours.

6. The client consults the psychic, not just for important decisions, but for *all* decisions, large and small. Example: "My husband wants to go to Tahiti for vacation, but I want to go to Greece. Where should we go?"

7. The client develops the perception that the psychic is their friend, family member, loved one, or soul mate.

8. The client comes to believe that they cannot survive without the assistance of the psychic.

9. The client is willing to sacrifice relationships with anyone who questions or critiques their dependency on the psychic.

10. The client is overly concerned with their psychic's evaluation of and approval of their decisions and actions.

11. The client is going into debt, is unable to pay their bills on time, or is chained to a job they do not like so they can afford the cost of seeing the psychic.

UNETHICAL RISK #3: FINANCIAL EXPLOITATION

As mentioned earlier, another danger for all psychics and healers is financial dependency. Emotional dependence often goes hand in hand with financial exploitation. When a client becomes dependent upon their psychic, they become vulnerable to financial exploitation. A client who feels they cannot live without their psychic will tend to spend large sums of money on readings regardless of whether or not they can afford them. An ethical psychic should discourage their clients from booking more sessions than they can afford. Avoiding emotionally dependent relationships with clients is one way to avoid getting into financially exploitative relationships with them.

The risk of financially exploiting clients occurs when we allow clients to pay for services that they do not need or that we are unable to deliver. One of the reasons that many people are suspicious of psychics is because some psychics have exploited the fears and vulnerabilities of clients for monetary gain. A well-known example of a tactic that some so-called psychics have employed is that of telling a client that they are cursed and then offering to remove the curse for a very large fee. Some of these same exploiters promise a client that they can bring them a marriage partner, a job, or a winning lottery ticket if they just pay a large sum of money for a special good luck charm, a magic candle, or a relic of some kind. Preying upon the fears and vulnerabilities of a client for monetary gain is financial exploitation.

An ethical psychic provides their services to help a client solve their problems, grow, and transform. The services the psychic provides should be helping the client become a happier, healthier person or have a happier, healthier, and more satisfying life. If your clients cannot afford your fee but insist on spending all of their money on you, you should dissuade them from doing so. If your fees are high, market your services to clients who can afford you.

In traditional training programs, these ethical risks are taught to students who are developing their gifts. Today, many students stumble across these risks while practicing. Consulting books like this one or joining organizations of spiritual communities that have a code of ethics can help the developing psychic avoid these risks. The Santeros Against Fraud and Exploitation (Orisha) and the Association of Independent Readers and Rootworkers (Hoodoo) are good resources for this work. Santeros Against Fraud and Exploitation (SAFE) has this to say:

> *[SAFE] is an action committee of the Santeria Church of the Orishas, dedicated to the exposure of deceptive practices and prevention of exploitation within the religion of Santeria. As an extension of our mission to educate, SAFE seeks to expose fraudulent practices to members of the public who may be uninformed about what is considered traditional, legitimate practice by the culture bearers of Santeria (Lucumi, Lukumi).*

In addition to educating the public about fraudulent practices we also firmly believe that a healthy religion is one that functions with transparency and adheres to a code of ethics. In an effort to spread ethical practice, the Santeria Church of the Orishas adheres with the Code of Ethics and Code of Conduct of the Association of Independent Readers and Rootworkers (AIRR—a subcommittee of the Missionary Independent Spiritual Church).[6]

AIRR is an organization for conjurers, root doctors, and Hoodooists, and it requires members to follow the code of ethics detailed on the SAFE website.

In addition to the code of ethics, both of these organizations also follow a code of conduct that requires that, among other things, ethical psychic readers and rootworkers not take advantage—financial or social—of clients who have psychological, medical, or legal problems. It is important, according to these codes, that no hidden fees or add-ons are added after the provider and the client agree upon a stated price for the services to be provided. They also discourage rootworkers from claiming that their spellcasting will always succeed or that it will produce results within a specific amount of time. They discourage making any guarantees.[7]

Figuring out what to charge a client can be tricky. Some traditional forms of healing don't require a set payment or else they only allow payment in kind. Typically, in these cultures, the healers are supported by the community so that they are free to help people without worrying about their needs being met. It is not that the healers are not paid, but rather that they are not paid directly by the sick. In other traditional cultures the fees for healing are quite high, and the high fee is part of what draws families together. When an entire family has to raise money or contribute goods and labor to effect a healing for a family member, it provides them with a way for the group to contribute to the healing of the individual by working together. The price of the healing is not what is important, instead it is the purpose for this price. Sometimes the fee is set high to ensure that the client will take the work seriously, which makes it more likely the healing will be successful.

Xhosa medicine woman Mercy Manci explains her approach to charging patients in the following way:

> *To help a patient, that is foremost in my mind, always . . . Some traditional healers become more concerned about what the patient can pay them. "Is this illness something that will require many treatments and herbs, so I will earn a good fee?" It is the wrong way around to practice. The patient comes first, the healing is first, a healer cannot concentrate on how much money they need to make. This way of looking at a patient and healing can confuse and even ruin a healer. It is not proper. The healing gift is from God and the ancestors. It is up to them to show us the way and provide for us. The ancestors are very clever and they will look after us if we treat this healing gift with great respect and humbleness.*[8]

UNETHICAL RISK #4: MAKING MATTERS WORSE

Psychics always run the risk of making matters worse for a client rather than helping them. An ethical psychic does everything in her power to help improve a client's situation and is vigilant about making sure this does not happen. In order to do this, the psychic must be attuned to the clients' needs and be aware of their weaknesses. She must be careful about what she says and how she says it. If the client walks away from the session feeling worse than she did when she arrived, the session was a failure. Sometimes the information that the psychic shares can be shocking or upsetting, disappointing, or unexpected. But, a psychic can find a way to dispense such information with compassion. For instance, you can remind the client of their agency, remind them that nothing is set in stone. You can encourage them to think about how this information can help them to grow, to change, or to achieve their goals.

Not all psychics will agree that we should strive to leave the client with hope no matter the message, but if your goal is to be a healer, if you are motivated by a desire to be of service, such considerations make sense.

Anytime the psychic gives bad news or provides an unwanted answer to a question the client asks, the potential exists for making the client feel worse. Because of the types of information that people typically consult a psychic for, the risk that the psychic will make matters worse is great. Often, people who are heartbroken, who are dealing with infidelity, divorce, lawsuits, illnesses, and other crises, go to psychics looking for answers. Clients sometimes ask questions of psychics without being prepared to hear the answers. These are some of the questions that clients ask that are rife with risk when answered:

1. Is my partner cheating on me?

2. Do I have cancer?

3. Am I going to have children?

4. Have I miscarried?

5. Is my child/spouse/family member going to die?

6. Am I going to die?

7. How long do I have?

8. Is she my soulmate?

9. Am I going to be successful?

10. Is he or she going to change?

11. Is my child going to be successful?

12. Will the murderer be found?

Some questions do not have good answers and the challenge that psychics face is in how and when to deliver bad news without making matters worse for the client. Balancing the need to be truthful with the need to be helpful is key to being an ethical psychic. Being sensitive to how much of the truth the client can handle and how best to deliver difficult truths in a way that clients can hear is an important aspect of being a good psychic.

If you must tell a client that their spouse is cheating on them, how will you do so? If a client has cancer, how will you tell them this? How will they handle it? Do they have a support system in place? If you don't tell the cancer patient about the cancer, are you preventing them from getting the treatment they need in a timely manner? Some psychics say you should always tell the truth, always answer questions fully. But is that what is best for the client? Because of the nature of the questions that clients bring to us, risks are entailed in answering them. The best way to handle these risks is to use your super senses to determine not only the answers to the questions but also to assess the client's readiness to hear certain answers.

Once I had a client who was severely depressed. She had come to me for a medical intuition scan to address a skin irritation. In the context of scanning for the cause of the condition I discovered the emotional component. Over a period of several health coaching sessions, I was able to get her to begin psychotherapy and to get tests run by medical doctors to diagnose the skin condition. In one of these sessions, she asked me if her husband was cheating on her. When I tuned in, I saw that he was having an emotional affair and that he was hoping it would lead to a sexual affair. When I tuned into her and her despair, I knew she could not handle the full story of his infidelity. I told her the truth—that he was flirting with a woman, but I did not tell her that I saw him sleeping with her in the future. I did not discuss his intent. A few sessions and a few weeks later, when she had worked on more pressing issues and was healthier, she asked me again about her husband. I told her more about his infidelity. Because she had resolved her more pressing health concerns—both physical and emotional—she was in a better place and better able to hear the bad news about her spouse.

If a psychic gives distressing news to someone who is already depressed, the results could be disastrous. The client might decide to take their own life in reaction to such bad news or the client might make a drastic decision or do something that cannot be undone. In situations in which I have found cancer in my client's body, I have often told them that they needed to see a doctor immediately, or that they needed to get a particular test or scan done to rule out cancer. I will sometimes tell a client that if they do not change their ways immediately they will develop cancer, or if I have to tell them they might have cancer, I am careful in how I word it. Sometimes, I will find that their condition is more dire than their doctors have indicated, and I will tell the client this. I may tell them to get a new doctor, or a second opinion, or not to wait a month for their next appointment. The important thing is to find a way to give them bad news that is empowering rather than disempowering.

I sometimes have clients who come to me for one thing that is not so serious and I find there is a much more serious thing they need to attend to. A client may be concerned that her partner is cheating on her sexually and I might find out that the partner is stealing from her. I may tell her the shocking news about the theft instead of discussing the affair because this may compel her to take action to protect herself and as a result she will be more empowered to handle the affair.

I once had a repeat client who was in danger. Her husband was going to kill her. I had to tell her. I saw what he had done in the past and described it to her; she confirmed that what I described had indeed transpired. I then told her she needed to leave as her life was in danger, and I gave her a detailed escape plan to secure the safety of her three children and herself. She was embarrassed, got upset, and complained to the owner of the healing center that my reading was too negative. But she had verified the accuracy of the reading already. She had told me that she was afraid he would kill her, but she was shocked that I knew and was embarrassed that she had, as I indicated, left him once but had gone back to him. Although my reading upset her, it did not make matters worse. Things were already as bad as they could be, and if I had not given her the bad news, she might have died.

I once had a client who came to see me for a clairvoyant reading and was asking about a business problem. In a strange turn of events his father (deceased) showed up in the reading to give the son business advice. After chatting with the father for a while and becoming convinced that the spirit who was delivering the messages through me was indeed his father, the son asked about his mother. His father showed me that his mother was very ill—deathly ill—and that she was going to die. The father was visiting her at night and taking her out of her body to go on astral traveling trips. He was preparing her for her death. The father told me that the mother was fine. She was ready to die, and everything was going to be okay. The father told me he was much more worried about the son than the mother.

In relating this information to the son, I did not relay all of it. I was tuned into the son and could feel his concern and worry for his mother even though he had not told me she was sick. I told him, "Your mother is very sick. I see her in a bed for a long time." "She has stage 2 cancer," he replied, "but the doctors say she can recover, perhaps with surgery. It's not advanced," he added. His words confirmed what I had already picked up. He was not ready to lose his mother and was in denial about the seriousness of her condition. He asked my advice about the treatment program. I told him what he needed to know about treatment options. I told him he needed to talk to her. I also told him to bring her to see me since I could not invade her privacy by discussing the severity of her condition with him without her permission. I did not tell him that she was ready to die because she needed to be the one to tell him that, not me. Telling him what I knew about her health would have been an invasion of her privacy and would have been too distressing for him. So, I was careful about what I told him and how I told it.

Fortunately, he listened to me and sent his mother to see me. When I started the medical scan on her, I found that I could not give her the usual information about possible treatments because it was clear that she did not want to fight the cancer and was not actually interested in treatments. She did not say this, but the information came through so clearly that I was blunt in saying, "You are not really interested in fighting this cancer, are you?" She stared back at me and stuttered. "Well," she started, ". . . my kids . . ." Her kids were all grown, and they wanted her to fight the cancer. She felt she had to go through the motions of pretending to fight because that was what they expected. As a part of the medical intuition scan, I visited the Akashic Records to determine the soul cause of the illness and was shown one of her past lives in which she sacrificed herself for her community. In that life she had thrown herself and her baby into a volcano as part of a deity sacrifice ritual. She had not wanted to sacrifice her life or the life of her baby, but she had done it for the community.

Before we are born, we make plans and decide on our life path. In her pre-life conference with her guide,[9] it was revealed that she had decided to do two things in the current incarnation: 1) She had made a contract with the soul of the baby she had been forced to sacrifice in the last life. She had promised to mother the child into adulthood in this life. This child was the son who had been my original client. 2) The second thing she had decided to do in this lifetime was to work on the lesson of making conscious decisions about life and death. In the previous life she had agreed to die for others rather than live for herself. In this life, she was being pressured to live for others when she wanted to die for herself. The soul wanted to learn how to make decisions consciously rather than allowing others to make decisions for her.

In this life, it was up to her whether she wanted to fight the cancer and live, fight the cancer and die, or not fight the cancer and die. In the case of the son, telling him his mother was going to die would have made matters worse. She needed to tell him. In the case of the mother, giving her a list of treatments and telling her she could beat the cancer if she wanted, while true, would have made matters worse.

Similarly, if a family member comes to you about an open investigation regarding a murder, a missing child, or a suspicious death, the information you give them can make matters worse. If you tell a parent that their missing child is dead or you tell a sister that her brother's death was not accidental but was the result of suicide, you could increase the grief of the family member. In such cases, the family needs the help of professionals in both crime and psychology. Are the parents of the missing child working with authorities? If they are, the psychic should try to work with the police who are investigating the crime. Otherwise, the information that the psychic provides will not be used and could further frustrate the family. Allison DuBois, a famous psychic detective, has warned psychics against working separately from the police.[10] Although many police departments are notoriously skeptical about the usefulness of psychics, more and more authorities are taking such sources of information seriously. If you give information to a family member about a victim, the family may decide to take matters into their own hands and put themselves (or their victimized family member, if they are still alive) in greater danger. A father may go after a murderer or a mother may try to locate and rescue her missing daughter and be killed herself.

It is not always easy to know what information will help a situation and what will make a situation worse. The psychic always risks making matters worse in delivering difficult information. The ethical psychic acknowledges and understands the risks and does all she can to avoid harm to her client.

INTERFERING WITH THE WILL OF OTHERS

The Power that we receive is for curing, healing, prophesying, solving problems, and finding lost people or objects. It is also for spreading love, transforming, and assuring peace and fertility. It is not to give us power over others because the source of power is not ourselves.

—FOOLS CROW, OGLALA LAKOTA HOLY MAN

The possession of power is always attended by the risk of abuse of that power. Psychics have power over non-psychics by virtue of their gifts and thus psychics must be ever vigilant in their wielding of their abilities: they must avoid controlling others. The risk of perverting the will of another with your gifts is perhaps the biggest risk that you will face as a psychic. Only by thoroughly understanding this risk and all the ways it can manifest in your work can you avoid it.

UNETHICAL RISK #5:
PERVERTING THE WILL OF ANOTHER

Using your gifts to influence someone's behavior in a particular direction, either with spellwork, with affirmations, as a guru, or otherwise, entails the risk of perverting the will of another. It is important for psychics to encourage their clients to become empowered and to make their own choices. It is imperative that the healer not make choices for clients that they should be making for themselves. As psychic-medium John Edward explains,

> *Every person you read for is vulnerable to some degree to your input and insights and is usually seeking direction. This direction is something that your clients have to figure out for themselves by using their own free will. You MUST NEVER tell them what to do, even if you believe you know what the personal outcomes will be for them. People have to learn their own "lesson" and it is not your job to stop them or get in their way.[1]*

As people with supersensory gifts, we must engage in our own self-government and self-restraint. To be psychic is to have access to power over others, and this responsibility must not be taken lightly. To be an ethical psychic, you must be vigilant in seeking to help and never harm.

A central tenet of witchcraft as practiced by true witches is what's known as the witches' rede: "And it harm none, do what you will." Those who are only dabbling in the art without formal training often overlook this moral law. Those who engage in filthy magic simply disregard it. According to a set of principles adopted by the Council of American Witches in 1974, "A witch seeks to control the forces within herself or himself that make life possible in order to live wisely and well without harm to others and in harmony with nature."[2]

Engaging in certain magical practices can put a psychic at risk of perverting the will of another. Psychics (some of whom identify as witches, brujas, or practitioners of magick may explicitly engage in certain forms of magic, telepathy, telekinesis, or energy work to control and influence people and circumstances. And although veteran practitioners of The Craft, Hoodoo, Brujeria, and other forms of magic will distinguish between good magic and filthy magic, hexes and juju, less practiced practitioners may not be able to so easily distinguish magic that harms from magic that is neutral or positive in its effects. Some psychics may not be aware that using their gifts to make things happen in someone else's life is wrong.

Some people mistakenly believe that traditions like Hoodoo, Vodun, Brujeria, and witchcraft have no ethics attached to them. This is often because of cultural appropriation and misrepresentation of these practices in the media. These days people watch videos and read books and imagine that they are voodooists and brujas. Because of cultural appropriation and commercialization of the traditions of Hoodoo/Conjure and Voodoo/Vodun by outsiders, it is hard to find books that discuss the ethical guidelines traditionally found in these traditions. Instead, there is an overabundance of Hoodoo spellbooks. Such books sell because they extract the practice from the culture. So people buy books on Hoodoo that tell them they can freely cast spells on people to get what they want. Most of these books are written by white authors, who have not actually been initiated into Hoodoo and who are merely seeking to make money. These people are not from the culture and they are often not trained in these traditions. Even some of the books written by Black authors are written in this way.

People initiated into Hoodoo do not reveal its secrets. Zora Neale Hurston, a prominent African American anthropologist who was one of the first Black authors to write about Hoodoo, was careful in her writings to leave out the most important aspects of the rituals. Because her work was funded by white philanthropists with certain agendas, she did include lists of spells in her writings, but anyone who knows the tradition knows she did not reveal anything important. She wrote about what her benefactors thought would sell, but she still safeguarded the secrets. Hurston was careful not to perpetuate stereotypes or reveal secrets in her writing about Hoodoo, but her writing did not correct misunderstandings or reveal the ethics of Hoodoo either. This is because her intellectual production was controlled, in part by the material interests of those who funded the research.

When traditions are removed from their cultural context and sold, they are never sold intact. One of the ways this has detrimentally affected the practice of Hoodoo and Conjure is that the extraction of the spells without the ethics has given many people free reign to engage in abusive psychic practices and to claim what they are doing is Hoodoo.

To understand Hoodoo and Voodoo, we must also consider the historical context. Both Hoodoo and Voodoo were developed in the context of slavery, when African-descended peoples were undergoing horrific torture, rape, and degradation—on a daily basis. As Hoodoo scholar Megan Lane explains,

> *Hoodoo Conjurers are cited often in accounts of the experiences of escaped slaves in historical narratives. Conjurers are identified as facilitators in the process of escape for slaves; one example is the commonly held belief that they could "Hoodoo the dogs" hunting for escaped slaves, causing them to stop and bark at trees while the person fled. Other Hoodoo practices in aiding escapees included rubbing graveyard dirt (Goopher Dust) onto the feet or footprints of the slave in order to prevent dogs from catching their scent.[3]*

African American conjurers/hoodooists, like Zora Neale Hurston's Uncle Monday, for example, were reputed to have greatly assisted the Seminole Tribe of Florida in winning its three wars against the United States.[4]

Brujeria was developed under colonialism and conquest in Latin America and the Caribbean. Hoodoo and Brujeria were primarily designed to assist these communities with survival, protection, self-affirmation, and pride. The people needed these methods to provide them with some protection from the evils of the enslavers, colonizers, priests, and landlords.

Because interpersonal racism and institutional racism still exist and continue to shorten the lives of Black and Brown peoples in the Americas, some of the protective spellcasting practices are still needed. Spells are not inherently bad, but they can be used to harm in circumstances where they are not warranted. As one hedgewitch explains,

> *[Spells] aren't entirely bad. Hexes are to teach a lesson and stop someone from continuing to do harm. Curses, on the other hand, are often employed to bring justice to a marginalized and otherwise ignored group when the system has failed them. For some, this is no different than the target going to jail or being executed for a crime. If you are hexing and cursing simply out of spite and the target's actions do not justify the punishment, then what you are doing is likely unethical.[5]*

Some of the hexes created in a historical context cannot be justified in the current one. Nor can they be justified when they are used against persons who are not engaged in evil. Yet—some practitioners still use them in this way. Similarly, in the past when women were so heavily oppressed by marriage and so dependent upon men financially, it made sense for them to develop love spells and hexes. Today some women have options and thus do not need to rely on spellcraft for their own survival or the survival of their children.

One modern-day curandera, Dr. Erika Buenaflor, talks about the use of *valaciónes* or candle petitions to shift outcomes in our lives without perverting the will of another. She writes:

> *[T]wo fundamentals must first be stressed. When writing the petition for a velación, (1) ask for an ideal outcome, and (2) understand that everyone has a right to their reality . . . I have . . .*

had a few clients throughout the years ask me, "Can't we make him or her understand, or do, XYZ?" Everyone has free will, so we cannot make anyone do anything if they are not willing. Nor can we make something happen to someone if there is no opening. Trying to do so . . . is often flat-out unethical. We can, however, ask for and have a right to our own ideal outcome.[6]

The use of affirmations is another instance in which a supersensory person can pervert the will of another. For example, Aquarian Age metaphysics, New Age doctrines, Religious Science, and Theosophy, to name a few, all encourage people to become aware of the power of thoughts and words. Members of these communities are taught to use thoughtforms and affirmations to make things happen in their lives. But some people are unaware of the difference between affirmations and incantations or spells.

An *affirmation* is a statement of something one wishes for or desires. Sometimes an affirmation is a message you are trying to give yourself by repeating a phrase over and over. "I am healthy," or "my life is peaceful and my relationships are harmonious," are examples of affirmations. But an *incantation* or *spell* involves using words magically to make things happen or influence other people. Some people believe that if they can make affirmations for their own life, they can also make them for other people's lives. But when you affirm that another person will or will not do something you want, you are no longer making affirmations. You are now making incantations. You are attempting, with your words, to abrogate the will of another. Affirmations, in the hands of a psychic, can become incantations or potent spells. An ethical psychic knows the difference and is careful not to replace affirmations with incantations that take away other people's free will.

A powerful psychic can also influence people during sleep or meditations. Edgar Cayce, a famous twentieth-century medical intuitive, once did a mental telepathy experiment to demonstrate to a skeptic that it could be done. He compelled men, who did not like him, to come to his office for no apparent reason. Psychics who know how to travel out of body consciously or exert their will through telepathy can do what Cayce did. After he had proved his point, Cayce said he would never conduct the experiment again because these examples of mental telepathy "show a forcing of yourself upon someone else . . . it pertains to the black arts." He continued, "It's one of those things none of us has a right to do unless we are very sure of what we are doing, and of our motives."[7]

What is necessary in evaluating the risks of magic is not simply affirming one's intention to "do no harm" but also affirming an awareness that perverting the will of another is almost always wrong. What right have you to affirm that your lover will always love you? What right have you to affirm that your child will always be obedient or that certain family members will follow your faith? Words have power, and when words are uttered by psychics, they are doubly powerful. As an ethical psychic, you are responsible for the words you utter, whether you call them affirmations, prayers, or incantations. If you are seeking to control another person's life with your words or rituals, you are perverting their will.

Some might argue that casting a spell on someone that causes them physical, financial, or emotional harm is wrong but that casting a love spell is fine because it is not harmful. But, this is not true. A love spell also involves perverting another's will. It involves forcing a person to do something that they would not otherwise do and this is wrong.

Another instance in which perverting the will can happen is when a psychic casts binding spells. A psychic may be tempted to bind a spell to or cast a spell upon a troublesome person if they suspect that person of harassing their client. Clients will frequently ask psychics to interfere in the lives of people they deem problematic. Although removing a spell or binding from your client is a good thing, casting a spell of binding on your client's enemy deprives the client's enemy of free will. An important distinction exists between defensive spells and offensive spells: a psychic has the right to protect themselves and others but should never control others, except in self-defense.

Sometimes, psychics use spells or charms to ensure business or make sure clients keep coming back. A known, unethical psychic, who claims to read the Akashic Records, inserts her own words into the voice of the Records in order to manipulate her clients into coming back to see her again and again. She has convinced a number of clients that they cannot live without her guidance. Reputedly she does this to guarantee financial success without regard for how she might be retarding the growth of her clients.

Another species of psychic exploits clients financially by scaring them with pronouncements that they are cursed; they then offer to remove the curse for a large fee, keeping their clients in a state of fear and dependency. Such clients come to think that their lives will not improve until the psychic frees them from the curse. The next time they experience a string of bad luck or unexpected misfortune, they assume they are cursed and need to spend more money on this psychic to free themselves.

Sometimes psychics engage in unethical behavior without being conscious of doing so. I had a client once who started having headaches and asked me to determine the cause. When I tuned in, I became aware that another healer was controlling this client and that one of the side effects was this headache. Not wanting to speak ill of another healer, I contacted two other psychic-healers I knew and asked them to tune in to either confirm or disconfirm what I was picking up. Both psychics confirmed that this healer was putting a "spell" on his clients to make them keep coming back to him. I had met this healer at a party earlier and saw him attempt to put a glamour spell on me so I would respect him.[8] At the time, I suspected that he might not have known what he was doing or that it might have been a reflex. That same healer later came to me for a medical intuition scan, and in his spiritual scan, I came across three past lives in which he had used his gifts to control others. In each of these lifetimes, he belonged to an oppressed group—women or disabled people—in societies that denied the group its basic rights. In these lives he had used his gifts to control others in order to address injustice and to improve the quality of life for those incarnations. He had carried the tendency to use his gifts in this way into this life. In the present incarnation, he did not need to use his gifts in this way because he was no longer experiencing the severe oppression he had faced in past lives. In fact, one of the lessons he had set up for himself in this life was to learn how to use his gifts ethically. It turns out he wasn't entirely aware of what he was doing; it was more of a habit he had developed over many lifetimes. But regardless of his consciousness about it, he was harming others. He was trying to compel people to come back to him for services. He didn't realize this could hurt people, that forcing them to come to him was not in their best interests, but he also wasn't making it his business to make sure he was not harming them. His priorities were askew and he needed more self-reflection. To be an ethical psychic, you must practice by the creed of the ancient Greek healer, Hippocrates, "First, do no harm."

Psychics are at great risk of harming their clients whether they use their gifts consciously to cast spells or enchantments or whether they unconsciously exert their will to overpower the client's will with words, affirmations, or teachings. Always remember: using your psychic gifts to manipulate others is wrong, regardless of the reason, and it incurs karmic debts. Because people who go to see psychics are often in crisis and are vulnerable to suggestion, it is possible for a psychic to talk a client into doing something that they normally would not do or that goes against what they believe. The psychic has a responsibility to consciously avoid engaging in such behaviors. As famed esoterica scholar Manly P. Hall explained so long ago, "We have reached a period in the history of the world when ignorance is criminal and deserves the heaviest penalty. Ignorance is not [filthy] magic, but it is the greatest ally that the [filthy] magician has in the world today."[9] Hall explains that "the [good] magician seeks to gain control over himself and the [filthy] magician seeks to gain control over others."[10] It is important for the practicing psychic to be aware of the dangers of perverting a will of another and to take steps to avoid doing so.

UNETHICAL RISK #6:
THE MISUSE OF SEXUAL ENERGY

Whenever two or more people connect sexually, they share and exchange sexual energy through their lower chakras. People who both love each other and have sex often connect through higher chakras as well. In a consensual exchange of energy, this sharing can be beautiful, pleasurable, inspiring, and solidifying for the aura. But in a nonconsensual exchange, the energetic effect is more akin to vampirism.

It is for this reason that the global pandemic of sexual assault and exploitation of women and girls by men (which also involves the solar plexus chakra) has taken such a toll on women. Because the lower chakras are associated with safety, security, and creativity—in addition to sexuality—unequal exchanges of sexual energy can cause trauma that has far-reaching energetic impacts. Abuses of sexual energy are not confined to sexual assaults. They also occur when someone is sexually manipulated, coerced, harassed, or sexually humiliated. The majority of sexual abuse that occurs in spiritual contexts is directed toward women, but other genders can also be targeted by the misuse of sexual energy.

In the case of psychics, psychic teachers, and supersensory gurus, a misuse of sexual energy can occur in less obvious and much more sophisticated ways. Sexual energy can be misused by anybody, but the risk of misuse is great for psychics and healers.

Because psychics are commonly using their gifts to access energy (and in the case of healers, to move and direct energy), they are at risk of misusing sexual energy and should take precautions. There are four ways that psychics and healers can misuse sexual energy:

1. As healers, they can stimulate the lower chakras during a healing session.

2. They can use their large auras to attract others and provoke crushes.

3. They can use their gifts to subvert the will of others and get them to return affection.

4. They can seduce people on the astral plane, during dreams or meditations, and this can lead to seduction on the physical plane.

The risk of using one's psychic gifts for sexual purposes and engaging in a misuse of sexual energy is greater for male-bodied psychics because of the current gendered power dynamic. However, all psychics must be vigilant. Persons with supersensory gifts have access to information that nongifted persons simply do not have. This gives the supersensory person an advantage in all relationships. Such an advantage necessarily creates a power dynamic that can be used to harm others, whether or not you intend to harm. Sexual relationships involve an exchange of sexual energy that is powerful and transformative, but this exchange can also be harmful. Sexual relationships involve vulnerability and surrender, and as a result, sexual energy exchanges that occur within the context of nonequal relationships come with the risk of doing harm.

Many energy healers: Reiki practitioners, sobadoras, shamans, medicine people, and others heal their clients by moving or removing energy in and from the client's aura. Cutting cords and removing thoughtforms, charms, spells, spirit attachments, and blocks in order to return the client to a state of wholeness is important healer work. However, while a person is receiving energetic adjustments of this kind, they are also open to energetic manipulation. Sexual manipulation through adjustments made to the lower chakras is easily accomplished by a talented healer with bad motivations or by one simply lacking in self-awareness. Every effort should be made not to excite or stimulate the sexual organs during a healing. If the healer finds that the client is experiencing sexual arousal, they should apologize and discontinue the session or redirect it to avoid creating sexual confusion or sexual dependence. Clients can experience sexual attraction to their healers and teachers without any energetic manipulation on the part of the teacher. Knowing this, the supersensory healer must take every precaution not to exploit this tendency. Knowing the risks in advance and taking every precaution to avoid accidental misuse of sexual energy during a healing is a requirement for every ethical psychic.

Psychically gifted persons who are also healers can emanate healing energy or possess large auras and this can influence the people who come into contact with them. People can become attracted to the healer's energy, and this attraction can be misinterpreted as or turned into a sexual attraction. As a result, healers may find that their clients and students are all attracted to them. They may find clients, students, and colleagues propositioning them, asking them out, or offering themselves to them. If healers act on these flirtations, they might find themselves sleeping with a large number of people, many of whom either admire them simply because of their gifts or who are attracted to their powerful auras. There is a reason that so many spiritual leaders throughout the ages have been accused of sexual impropriety. Managing this risk is a huge responsibility for the ethical psychic.

It would be a mistake for supersensory persons to listen to ego and assume that they are sought after because they are charming or attractive. A supersensory person can be physically unattractive, lack charm or intelligence, and still attract admirers. People don't want to sleep with you because you are physically irresistible; they want to sleep with you because you are energetically irresistible.

Although the risks of unconscious misuse of sexual energy are many, psychics can also consciously misuse sexual energy with their thoughts and wishes. This is why we often see gurus, ministers, and spiritual leaders accused of sexually exploiting their followers/congregations/students. Because of the power dynamic that can obtain between supersensory persons and regular persons, this risk is always there. This risk affects all psychics, not just professional practitioners, healers, spiritual leaders, or gurus. A psychic can intentionally or unintentionally cast spells on the object of their lust or affection and thus unfairly influence romantic partners. In fact, the two most common ways psychics can use their gifts to pervert the will of another are through sexual and financial control.

Sexual exploitation is not as common as financial exploitation, but it is a serious risk for the highly gifted. A highly gifted person can use their gifts to influence people to their own advantage through various means. One famous spiritual leader in California who presides over a very large spiritual community is a prime example of this misuse. Within this community, he targets women for sexual predation and seduction. He is able to convince women (and sometimes men) who would normally never be interested in him, either because they are married or much younger than he is, to sleep with him, fall in love with him, and even leave their marriage partners for him. He does not get these women simply because he is handsome or brilliant or charming or kind. Most people would not be willing to commit adultery, change their sexual orientation, or date a man older than their father, even if he did have a long list of wonderful traits. Instead, this psychic and healer misuses his psychic gifts to attract sexual partners. He does this by beginning his seduction on the astral plane. He visits his victims on this plane where he plants the seeds of their physical union. He connects with them out of body, during meditation, in dreams, and in church services. Sometimes he even connects with them sexually on the astral plane. After he visits them repeatedly in what they remember as particularly vivid dreams, these people come to feel that they have a significant otherworldly connection with him and that they are meant to be together. The combination of the fact that he is a spiritual leader with the fact that these experiences occur during spiritual activities (like meditating, church services, or retreats) can cause the victim to feel that these out-of-body experiences are spiritual experiences of great significance.

Thus prepped, the victims come to see the physical sex act as more significant than merely an expression of lust or even of love. Instead, they view it as having a cosmic or spiritual significance. The victim considers herself special for having been chosen, but beyond that, she comes to think the relationship is fated, a part of a grand design, God's will, or preordained by a soul plan or contract. Because these women have likely never before had an affair with someone who visited them in their dreams and meditations, or who sent them telepathic messages, they do not know how to process the experience or protect themselves from it. And more often than not, the only framing they have for how to interpret it comes from the teachings of the very same person who is seducing them.

Although the spiritual practitioners who are guilty of misusing sexual energy are most often men, women can also use sexual energy to seduce their students and clients in their roles as spiritual advisors, psychics, or healers. Some students have asked me how such behavior can be detected. The proof of such visits happening can be found in the way the appearance and behavior of the seduced or charmed individual changes. Repeated astral visits by a supersensory teacher can have a powerful effect on a person. They can become completely disarmed and can appear to fall into what looks almost like a hypnotic trance. When they decide to have an affair with someone they would normally not be attracted to and engage in acts that violate their core moral principles, it is obvious that the spiritual leader is taking away their free will. The victim may think they are making their own choices, but these choices will not appear to comport with their values or best interests. The victim may also talk of these transcendent experiences they have had with the psychic and offer these as proof that their union is a part of Divine Order.

A person lacking in super senses may be unable to detect a "spell," "charm," or any other form of sexual manipulation cast on them, and thus they will find them difficult to resist. This, once again, gives the psychic an unfair advantage over the nongifted person, and for this reason such an interaction is extremely unethical. As stated throughout this book, a psychic must guard against the temptation to use their abilities to hold power over other people. Overpowering someone sexually, through magical force, means you do them great harm that can have lasting traumatic impacts. Such harm is soul-level and has the potential to impact multiple incarnations. In the physical realm, healing from sexual harm can sometimes take generations, and in the nonphysical realm it can take multiple lifetimes.

All forms of perverting the will of another can affect one karmically, but controlling another person sexually has an especially powerful effect given the harm it produces to the victim's energy. Supersensory persons must take great care to avoid misusing sexual energy because perverting the will of another sexually is far worse than perverting the will of another for financial gain, though both activities create karmic debts for the psychic involved. If you harm a person in this life, you may feel compelled to heal that person in another life. You may set up certain karmic debts that you will feel you must fulfill in subsequent incarnations. The ethical psychic takes great care to do their own internal work to avoid any temptation to subvert the will of another.

FAKE GURUS

There has always been a proliferation of fake gurus and fake shamans using their gifts to exploit unsuspecting seekers. As we've discussed in this chapter, two of the biggest risks for a psychic teacher are perverting the will of another and misusing sexual energy. The fake guru is an example of a psychic teacher who is often guilty of both.

Fake gurus are supersensory teachers who use their gifts to control others. Teachers of healing and psychic arts and spiritual leaders with psychic gifts are all at risk of becoming fake gurus. Real gurus do exist, but fake gurus are more prevalent, at least outside of India. Fake gurus and shamans are particularly dangerous because they often engage in perverting the will of another, misusing sexual energy, and cultural appropriation, all at once. This is why an aspiring spiritual teacher or leader faces so many risks.

In India and other parts of Asia, a *guru* is a respected spiritual teacher who guides and initiates their followers on a particular spiritual path in life. "In the Vedic tradition, a guru was a reputed priest (brahmana) who performed purification ceremonies and initiated young students into the study of the Vedas. In ancient India, spiritual teachers taught the higher knowledge of the Vedas."[11] But what happens when the idea of a guru is transplanted to the US? When the teacher is taken out of the cultural context? It then becomes very easy for the idea of the guru to become corrupted.

Numerous ancient texts in India spell out the traits of a guru, but modern-day gurus are not all based in India and they are not all educated in the ancient traditions that gave birth to the guru tradition. Even those who are so educated often travel to Western countries and depart from the ancient traditions. They become addicted to the adulation, wealth, and devotion of others. Some Eastern Gurus come to the West precisely because they know they will not be held to the same high moral standard they were held to in their home country. There have been gurus who have come to the United States from the East and have ceased to behave as true gurus, becoming instead corrupted fake gurus who collect material goods, seduce followers, and hypocritically demand sacrifices from their followers that they themselves have either never practiced or have ceased to practice. The traits of a fake guru are not the traits of a true guru. A true guru

> *should be knowledgeable, self-realized, liberated (jivanmukta), chaste, virtuous, austere, truthful, detached, free from lust and delusion, and dedicated and devoted to God. He [or she] should be wise, absorbed in God, selfless, egoless, humble, indifferent, but firm in enforcing discipline through personal example. A true guru practices renunciation in word and deed and remains the same to all the dualities of life. He shuns fame, name, wealth, ownership, publicity, worldly pleasures, luxuries and public attention.*[12]

Some fake gurus are Westerners who have culturally appropriated the whole notion of guruhood from a culture that is not their own. Westerners have long had a fascination with what they call "The Orient" and have been engaged in various forms of cultural appropriation for centuries. Westerners struggle to understand how to be a guru because we lack the centuries-long tradition that birthed the guru in the East. Then too, cultural appropriation is characterized by the tendency of colonizers and their descendants to extract aspects of a culture that they can use for their own gain and leave the rest, deeming it unimportant. Thus, a Westerner may like the trappings of a guru community but may not be interested in the discipline required to participate in such a community.

True gurus are characterized by humility, tolerance, compassion, and renunciation, and this is what makes them uniquely qualified to teach their followers how to develop such traits. In authentic guru communities, the focus is on spirituality, not business or materialism. Discipline is expected of followers because the guru is a model of discipline. Gurus are followed because they have a demonstrated amount of training or education and experience with a tradition. They are also followed because of their wisdom and/or gifts. Gurus are not like other people. They are uniquely qualified, by their own gifts, knowledge, and wisdom to lead others. A true guru's reputation precedes them. Many people can testify to their character. A true guru will not need to be boastful or proud; their followers and students will speak of the guru's accomplishments and how they have positively impacted their students. A true guru or teacher does not financially or sexually exploit their students. Traditionally, studying with a guru involves a lot of discipline. The guru is able to demand such discipline because they have already devoted many years to a disciplined life.

A Westerner may go and study with a guru on holiday or on weekends for a short amount of time and then decide that they are ready to be a guru and begin gathering their own students or followers. Cultural appropriators pick and choose those aspects of a cultural practice they want to adopt. They often leave behind the more challenging aspects such as discipline, rigor, self-renunciation, and so on. They take shortcuts, failing to benefit from the full instruction, and thus they are inadequately trained for the work of a true guru. Fake gurus model themselves after true gurus but fail to adhere to the moral strictures prescribed for such roles.

Fake shamans culturally appropriate Indigenous traditions of healing in order to obtain status and financial gain.[13] The status that each of these roles brings to the psychic sets them up to have power over large groups of people. *Shaman* is a term that refers to a wide variety of medicine people and healers in Indigenous cultures throughout the world. A real shaman is chosen or called to the work and does not choose it, pay for it, or make it a career path. As Navajo shaman Don Hoskie explains, "You can't choose to be a medicine person. You must be chosen."[14] A shaman will either become very ill, have a near-death experience, or begin to have dreams or behave in strange ways as a young person. Certain signs and symbols will lead a person to accept their role as a shaman. Sometimes they are sick and cannot get better until they accept their role. Shaman work usually requires sacrifice, and many people resist the call because living the life of a medicine person or shaman is never easy. Fake shamans read books or take courses and call themselves shamans. They were not chosen, they were not born with gifts, they were not called by a dream or identified by an elder shaman. They just decided to be shamans because they think it is interesting or fun or that they can make money from it.

Whether a person is a fake guru or a fake shaman, they are in a position to cause harm because either they are not following the discipline of a guru or they have not been chosen as a shaman. As a result, they make their own rules, guided by ego rather than service, typically do whatever they want, and are not bound by principles that have either been passed down in a tradition or given by revelation.

A fake guru can be helpful to their students and still harm them. It is unlikely that so many fake gurus would be so successful if they were not capable of providing true assistance to their students and clients. Most do help people. Many can transform a person's life. Unfortunately, the work often does not end there. They exact a price for their healings and teachings that is energetic rather than financial. They require energetic dependency, or control of their students' lives, or that their students give themselves sexually to them.

Even if a teacher, healer, or psychic does not charge money for their services, energy is always exchanged—either explicitly or in unspoken ways. Gurus who do not tell you what the exchange will be may surprise you later with what they expect in return for what you have gained from them.

I knew a healer once whose teacher provided her with incredible healing. Before becoming a healer, the student had suffered from serious mental health issues. As a result of her own tenacity and her work with her teacher, she had begun to live a normal life and she was no longer spending time in mental hospitals, taking pharmaceuticals for her problems, or experiencing psychotic breaks. The help she received from this teacher was immense and undeniable. However, by this point, the teacher had begun to control every aspect of her life. The teacher told her what classes to take, how to run her business, who to date, and how to interact with her children. She had the teacher on speed dial and consulted her throughout the day requiring advice on every detail of her life. The teacher regularly encouraged her to break off relationships with anyone who questioned her devotion to the teacher. And the teacher encased the student in a bubble of energy protection that on the surface seemed to be a good thing; however, it became apparent that this bubble of protection also prevented her from receiving healing or teaching from anyone else. This maintained her dependency on just one teacher and thus limited her continuing growth.

I had a colleague once who was a former cult member. In the ashram in which she lived, the guru controlled every aspect of the financial and sexual lives of his students. He required celibacy from them until marriage, claimed to be celibate himself, and chose marriage partners for those who wanted to marry. Nobody was allowed to have sexual relations without his permission and students found to violate the celibacy rule were ejected from the community. Students were taught to think of this as a form of self-renunciation that would help to further their spiritual growth. Because the guru was from India, his followers, largely European-American, trusted his structures. They assumed they were authentic. Meanwhile, the guru developed sexual relationships with a number of his female devotees behind closed doors. He used energy work to stimulate their lower chakras during healings and effected kundalini orgasmic experiences in them. He then had intercourse with them, claiming he was giving them orgasms through "shakti energy." He told them these sex acts were a part of their spiritual development, and most believed him.[15]

Because my future colleague was in a cult, she and other students had cut off all ties with family and friends. They had quit their jobs and worked for the guru for free or without much compensation, and they had given all of their savings to him. They were totally dependent upon him so that when some women finally decided to speak out about the sexual abuse, they risked losing everything. The community was eventually disbanded when officials got involved, and the students were set adrift without the resources or community ties they needed to support themselves. During their time in the cult, they also lost the ability to think for themselves or to operate fully in society. Instead of becoming the spiritually advanced or the healthy whole people they were meant to be, they had become dependent in every way.

Numerous American gurus and appropriative practitioners been charged with the sexual and/or financial abuse of their followers, and some abuses have even led to injury or death. Some of the more famous cases include Shri K. Pattabhi Jois ("Guruji"), founder of Ashtanga yoga; Bikram Choudhury, the founder of Bikram or Hot Yoga; and Swami Satchidananda, of Woodstock fame who were all accused of rape and sexual abuse by several of their followers.[16] In recent years white fake shaman James Arthur Ray was convicted for the death of three of his students who died during a fake sweat-lodge ceremony in Sedona.[17]

In Hindu culture, traditional gurus have had and continue to have so much power over their followers that it is always possible that their position can be corrupted. Traditionally students were expected to serve gurus in particular ways:

A guru's word is inviolable. He is the door keeper of the secret knowledge, which is hidden in the scriptures. He has the right to choose his students and initiate them into the transcendental knowledge according to his discretion. No one can benefit from his teachings without paying him their dues (guru dakshina). Paying respects to a guru, touching the feet of a guru,

serving the guru and taking care of his personal needs, prais-
ing and appreciating a guru, seeking the blessings of a guru,
remembering and meditating on the name of a guru are part
of Hindu spiritual tradition.[18]

But "taking care of the personal needs" of a guru can be perverted into taking care of the sexual needs of a guru. Allowing
the guru to initiate his students "according to his discretion" can
devolve into bizarre and abusive initiatory practices. Paying the
guru their dues can be interpreted as turning over all their assets.
When being provided access to "the door keeper of the secret
knowledge," a student can be required to do many things.

Hypocrisy is one of the signs of a fake guru or a spiritual teacher
with cult tendencies; in other words, such leaders do not follow
the precepts they have outlined for their students. For example,
they tell their students they must confine their sexcapades to only
one partner chosen by the leader, but then they take multiple
wives for themselves. Such a guru tells his students that they must
go without sleep or food or comforts in order to prove their devotion, but then the guru lives in a mansion with servants, eats rich
foods, wears fine silks, and sleeps as much as they like.

An Indian guru, Shri Mataji Nirmala Devi, has spoken a lot about
false gurus. She explains that a false guru "leads a very funny life,
immoral life." She continues: "A person who himself is not pure has
no business to make others pure. There are many things described
about false gurus in our scriptures, thank God. And so, if you see
their behavior, . . . they say something and do something else."[19]

At its extreme, the abuses perpetuated by a fake guru or
shaman result in them starting their own cult. Cults have particular features, and once a person becomes aware of these, it becomes
easier to identify and avoid them. Cults are usually run by charis-
matic leaders (aka fake gurus), who require their members to cut
outside ties with friends and family. The guru often controls the
lives of the members, including where and how they live, what

kind of work they do, how they manage their finances, and who they sleep with or marry.

Most of us imagine that cults are founded only by narcissists and other types of sociopaths and that well-meaning people don't start cults. We might also assume that only people who are insecure or emotionally damaged in some way ever join cults, but we would be wrong in both of these assumptions. Although it is true that some of the more famous, more dangerous cults have been started by sociopaths who thrive on controlling others, not all cults are malignant in origin, and not all cult members are broken in some way before they join a cult. The traits that make cult leaders successful do not just include their ability to manipulate people for their own purposes. This is why you don't have to be a fool to be taken in by a cult. Cults succeed because they offer their followers something of extreme value—whatever members receive is so extremely valuable that once they receive it, they find it very difficult to walk away. Cult leaders are often psychically gifted individuals who may also be smart and charming. They know what people want and need, and they are very good at providing it. They differ from other spiritual teachers and guides in that they are ultimately more interested in getting their own needs met than meeting the needs of their flocks.

The fake gurus or cult leaders likely to cause the most damage are those with supersensory abilities. Psychic abilities confer power onto psychics, whether they seek it out or not. How you handle that power determines what kind of psychic, healer, or guru you might become.

As Lord Acton once wrote, "Power corrupts and absolute power corrupts absolutely."[20] Power is seductive, and not everyone can handle the seduction of power once they have it. A person with psychic power has the ability to have power *over* others. You might start out thinking that your mission is a good one, your purpose might be lofty, and you might try to justify manipulating others, convincing yourself that it is for the greater good. But an ethical psychic always enters into her work conscious of the seductive effects of power. She takes necessary steps to avoid using her power to control others. She discourages her students from handing over too much power and judiciously avoids manipulating her students or clients either intentionally or unintentionally.

Being a good psychic or healer is not simply about helping others, intending to help others, or having evidence that you have helped others. Nor is it simply about intending to do good or intending not to harm. To be an ethical psychic, you have to be vigilant and continuously assess whether any of your actions or behaviors are harming any of your students, regardless of your original intent. There must be self-reflection. You must constantly search for signs of arrogance or feelings of omnipotence. You have to be preemptive and proactive in seeking to do no harm. You have to make this a conscious choice and repeatedly question your motives. An ethical psychic would never use her gift to control the will of another or to misuse sexual energy. Ethical psychics do not become fake gurus because they are ever conscious of these risks.

4

WORKING WITH SPIRITS AND SOUL PATHS

There is [a] frequently exercised influence which may seriously retard a disembodied entity . . ., and that is the intense and uncontrolled grief of his surviving friends or relatives. . . . we not only cause ourselves an immense amount of wholly unnecessary pain over this temporary parting from our loved ones, but we often also do serious injury to those for whom we bear so deep an affection by means of this very regret which we feel so acutely.[1]

—CHARLES W. LEADBEATER

Being an ethical psychic involves taking care with how you interact with others and this extends to others in the Other World. Interactions with spirits are fraught with all kinds of risks. Some risks, like that of interfering with the will of another, extend to spirits as well as humans. But interaction with spirits can also expose the psychic and the client to risks in the form of unwanted harassment by earthbound spirits and the creation of portals. The ethical psychic must take all of these risks into account before helping clients with issues related to spirits.

UNETHICAL RISK #7:
CONTROLLING THE DESTINY OF SOULS

Special care must be taken not to control spirits when working with them. Whenever a psychic medium works with a spirit, she risks influencing the destiny of a soul, both the living and the dead. A medium that calls spirits in to deliver messages to humans may inadvertently affect the destiny of the deceased souls.

For example, I have sometimes had situations where I called a spirit at the behest of their relative only to discover that the spirit was otherwise occupied with more important activities. In some cases, spirits are busy healing or recovering from their own Earth life. Spirits have a number of options after they die. If they died by suicide or tragically in some manner, they go to healing and rehabilitation rooms. Others attend spirit school. Although Earth is considered the most advanced school, many spirits study in spirit schools before and after they study in the Earth school of life. A spirit who is in school has a teacher and classmates, and as with Earth school, they are expected to attend class and to pay attention to the lesson. So calling a spirit away from school or work on the Other Side is no small thing. Sometimes they can leave off what they are doing to join us on the Earth plane, and sometimes they cannot or should not. It is usually more important for deceased spirits to work on their own evolution than it is for them to answer our Earth questions, and until deceased spirits complete their life reviews, they cannot move on. Spirits who are too preoccupied with their surviving relatives or the affairs on Earth related to their death may be unable or unwilling to attend their life review or complete their healing on the Other Side, which is the real danger of calling spirits down to Earth who have better things to do with their time. If such spirits are routinely interrupted and called down to Earth to involve themselves with the concerns of the living, they may fall behind in their spirit studies or their own soul's progress. Of course, not all mediums have the ability to compel spirits to come when they call. Some psychic-mediums may try to call specific spirits for their clients and find they are unable to do so. But for those who *are* capable of compelling spirits to come, the risk is real; the ethical psychic takes this responsibility very seriously.

Sometimes, coming to Earth to talk to relatives and friends *is* beneficial for the departed soul and actually helps them to move on. Sometimes participating in resolving the problems of loved ones who are still living helps the spirit provide the service that their souls are yearning for. Twice I have had young souls be allowed to spend time talking to their surviving relatives after passing precisely because they needed to deal with the effects of their decisions to either die by suicide or to recklessly throw away their lives. The healing of the deceased and the healing of the survivors can sometimes happen at the same time when a conversation is facilitated between the two sides. But, if returning to Earth is not healing for the spirit, it should be avoided because it could be injurious and could negatively impact the destiny of the soul.

The risk of controlling the destiny of souls, both living and "dead," is real, and the unethical psychic can delay the progress of souls, whether or not they are occupying physical bodies. The living can become stuck in their grief, stuck in the past, stuck in their problems, and can become unable to move forward. A medium who allows her client to request that they contact the same deceased relative again and again, without a clear need, can retard the growth of both the client and the deceased relative or spirit. For example, the client may fail to learn the lesson they are supposed to be learning from their grief—sometimes the client needs to let the spirit go and move on with their life. A client who visits a psychic-medium to talk to the same deceased loved one repeatedly can become stuck. The deceased relative can also become stuck, preoccupied with helping their surviving relative process the grief instead of attending to their own growth needs. In this way, the psychic-medium can negatively impact the destiny of the client's soul and/or the soul of the deceased.

I once had a client who lost his daughter to suicide. He could not get over his daughter's sudden and very brutal death. He came to me several times to speak with his daughter about her passing. The first couple of sessions were helpful. He was able to clear up some of the family's questions regarding why his daughter had done what she did. It turned out that she had an undiagnosed mental illness. Explaining this to the father was healing for him. However, at a certain point, it was clear that my client's attachment to his daughter was holding both him and his daughter back. The father spent all of his time trying to communicate with his deceased child in meditation and stopped communicating with his wife; as a result, his marriage dissolved.

I felt the father would be better off if he could let his child continue on her path, and I offered to help send the spirit to the light. But the father wasn't ready to send his daughter on her way. He liked feeling her presence at different times and places throughout the day. The daughter's guides informed me that it was okay for her to stay a little longer and assured me that she was learning by witnessing the destruction of her family that had resulted from the suicide. Witnessing this was helping the spirit to grow spiritually. However, they said, at a certain point, the spirit would need to move on to the next level of her own development—healing, her life review, spirit school, and so on. If her father refused to let her go at that time, the father would be delaying her soul growth. Because of the daughter's own feelings of guilt and regret, she would likely stay with the father for as long as the father needed her to, as a way of doing what she perceived as her penance, even if such continued penance was neither required nor beneficial.

Holding on to the child's spirit was also preventing the father from dealing with his earthly life. He had a wife and another child who needed his attention, but he failed to nurture these relationships and simply withdrew into his grief, allowing himself to be comforted only by his dead daughter's spirit. He failed to learn or grow and entered, for a time, a state of stagnancy. At a certain point I had to stop doing mediumship sessions with him and I changed the focus of our sessions to life coaching so that he could begin to move on and to heal his life. I informed him that letting his child go needed to be one of his goals and that it would not be appropriate to keep calling the daughter down for sessions.

In another case, I worked with a client who had lost his sister to suicide. I did three sessions with the client to help him process her sudden death. During these sessions I also worked with the "dead" sister to help her progress on the Other Side. When she had progressed to a point where she was busy in her spirit lessons on the Other Side, I no longer held sessions for him with her as it would have interrupted her soul growth.

A psychic who provides guidance to a client who is dealing with relationship problems also risks retarding the growth of the client. Many relationship problems that people encounter in their lives are the result of karmic contracts they have made with other souls or groups of souls. A psychic not attuned to the bigger picture—if, for example, they have no access to Higher Self/Soul information about the person—may advise the client to leave their partner, cut off ties with their family, or leave their job simply because doing so will immediately decrease the stress the client is feeling. However, sometimes stress is a necessary part of growth. People actually "sign up" for difficult relationships before they are born because such relationships help them or their fellow souls to grow in important ways. People who decide to just stop communicating with difficult siblings, parents, or lovers might be missing out on completing an important soul contract.

Similarly, if a psychic allows their personal beliefs to influence the guidance they give, they may inadvertently obstruct the growth of their client. For example, a few clients have come to me because they found themselves in love triangles that went against their expectations and they were conflicted about what to do. At least one of them told me that the last psychic she had been to was so disapproving of the fact that she was dating a married man that she was unable to give her any useful guidance. In 75 percent of the clients I have had who were involved in adulterous affairs, the forbidden relationships were the direct result of a soul contract. In these cases, the soul was learning valuable lessons in the context of these forbidden relationships, and in two such relationships, the soul was supposed to be with the forbidden person rather than with the person with whom they had made an earthly vow. If psychics allow themselves to pass judgement on infidelity, or any other life choice, they can lose their ability to see what their clients actually need.

Because I access the Akashic Records I am able to get soul-level information. As souls, we make plans that, when played out on the Earth plane, do not always conform to societal expectations and norms. In one case, a woman came to me while she was having an extramarital affair. If she had been my friend asking me for advice, I might have told her it was wrong to lie and break her vows. I might have shared with her my own experience of being cheated on and explained to her how much it hurt to have that trust betrayed. But she did not come to me as a friend. She needed advice from a higher level.

When I accessed the client's book in the Hall of Records, I discovered that she was meant to form a partnership with the lover because he was going to help her step onto her life path. Her husband had played a particular role in her life, but they had both completed their contracts. At this time in her life, she was meant to begin a new path, and the new man was a part of that new spiritual path. It was time for her to end the first relationship and begin her spiritual work. This second man agreed in a soul contract to appear at this time to remind her of her spiritual path.

In another case of adultery, I encountered two souls who were caught up in trying to redo a relationship from a past life. In the past life, they had been fellow soldiers and best friends and one of them had protected the other. They had died together in that life and thus had a very strong soul link. In this life, they felt an intense attraction to and familiarity with one another and this resulted in an affair. In the past life they had been telepathic; in this life, they were also telepathic. Because of these strong ties, they both had a hard time breaking off the adulterous affair. But they were not destined to be together romantically. The soul of the married man had contracts with his spouse and children that required that he stay married. Although the client was correct in saying that they were soulmates, she was not right in assuming that he was supposed to leave his family to be with her. In these and other cases, I had to disregard either my own beliefs or those of the client in order to deliver the needed information.

Another way a psychic can negatively impact the destiny of a soul is by foretelling the future. Psychics must be very careful about the prophecies they make and ought to be careful not to give clients the impression that the future is set in stone or predetermined. Human beings always have choices. Because psychics have access to information that non-psychics do not, they run the risk of having clients listen to everything they say and follow their advice very literally. It is the job of the psychic to remind the client that their life choices are theirs and that the future is not set. Instead, a psychic can provide predictions for the future based on if/then statements. For example, a psychic can tell a client that "if you continue on this path, then this will happen." Or "if you don't make substantial changes in your dietary habits, you will get sick." "If you and your mate don't get couples counseling, separate, move, talk about a certain issue, then you will get divorced." "If you get that surgical procedure, then you will not recover." If/then predictions provide information and guidance about the future without abrogating the client's free will; they allow the client to take charge of their future instead of feeling controlled or overwhelmed by it.

Encouraging clients to take sovereignty over their lives elimi-
nates the risk of perverting their will. Ultimately the ethical psychic must encourage their clients to trust themselves and to learn
how to listen to their own intuition. If a client becomes dependent
upon coming to a psychic repeatedly and refuses to take charge of
their life, their growth can be retarded. If, for example, the client
comes to the psychic to avoid making their own decisions or is
coming for reasons other than personal transformation, the session could simply provide them with an excuse to not address their
own problems. A frequent example of this is when a client needs
psychotherapy but instead goes to a psychic in an effort to avoid
dealing with emotional issues. The psychic who continues to see
such a client instead of recommending therapy risks retarding the
emotional growth of the client.

UNETHICAL RISK #8: CREATING DISHARMONY
THROUGH PORTALS AND POSSESSION

Psychics who work mediumistically have to concern themselves
with the risks that attend dabbling in other realms. Although most
mediums tend to bring through deceased loved ones, any time a
psychic steps into the Other World, they chance coming into contact with a whole range of beings, not all of whom are harmless.
When the psychic/medium enters the spirit world they risk creating
disharmony that can harm the living. Although our deceased loved
ones usually do not intend to harm us, a special category of beings
called *earthbound spirits* can harm us intentionally or otherwise.

Earthbound Spirits

Earthbound spirits are the spirits of humans who once lived on
Earth but who now lack bodies and have failed to follow the normal
trajectory for leaving the Earth plane, such as "moving toward the
light" and into the Other World where they can review their most

recent life, meet with relatives, teachers, and guides, and embark on new lessons. Such spirits are often unwilling to leave the Earth plane because they have excessive attachments to some aspect of earthly life; this may be an attraction to a person, to their things, or to an addiction to food, sex, or drugs. Such attachments keep them bound to Earth in a frustrating pattern of seeking, again and again, to satisfy their desire to enjoy and/or participate in earthly things that they can no longer enjoy. Such earthbound spirits can wreak havoc in the lives of the living. They don't just come for a visit to reassure their family that they are okay. They feel a need to stay attached to the Earth plane and, as is the case for human addicts, they often don't take into account how their need to satisfy their cravings might negatively impact others.

The psychic-medium runs the risk of spirit attachment in calling on a deceased relative to converse with a living person; the spirit called might feel they are so needed on Earth that they decide not to leave after the reading. They might actually attach themselves to the living relative. Spirit attachment, regardless of the original intent of the spirit or the psychic, is rarely good for any of the souls involved. Often when an earthbound spirit is attached to a living person, the human loses their free will and is prevented from living the life they might have otherwise lived.

A client once came to me to have a session with his deceased father. I did not need to call the father to come talk to us because he was already there. He hovered in his son's aura, still angry about his illness and death. He had suffered from the slow decline that comes with a degenerative disease and he had died angry and frustrated with his disabled body. He refused to move on because of his anger and because he wanted his son to continue to take care of him, even after death, as he had when he was ill. Although he had several children, this son was the one he had always called. Strong bonds during life, negative or positive, can lead to attachments after death.

In the session, I made the spirit aware of the light and called in the angel orderlies to help him to the Other Side. After he left, my client felt so relieved. He said he had felt all of this anger and did not know why. After the session it became clear that the anger belonged to the father, not the son. Because the father had been attached to him, the son was being overshadowed with the father's heavy emotions. It wasn't until the father left that my client was freed of that oppressive emotion.

Earthbound spirits frequently share addictions with their surviving relatives. I have come across a fair number of alcoholics and drug addicts who had spirit attachments to alcoholic/addicted relatives. Having these attachments caused them to be heavily influenced by cravings that were not their own. Such attachments can make it difficult for these people to become sober because their will is being perverted by the will of the deceased. Because attachments are potentially so damaging, they must be discouraged as much as possible and removed by those trained to do so.

Spirit attachment, when taken to an extreme, can result in spirit possession. When a spirit takes possession of a person, they can completely control the individual. Sometimes souls who have passed on but who are still addicted to some physical aspect of life will seek to possess a living person so that they can fully experience life again. Possession is the most extreme form of a violation of free will and is an extreme form of disharmony between worlds. When a soul loses her body to a possessing spirit, she can no longer fulfill her life purpose. The soul who does the possessing is also retarding their growth by cheating their way into another lifetime instead of doing the Other World work required before incarnating again.

I once had a client who met with me regularly to contact a relative who had died and left some financial issues unresolved. These unresolved issues were causing a lot of family conflict and the spirit was able to help the family by meeting with us and answering questions.

Spirits are often eager to come meet with mediums if there is some chance they can help their surviving friends and/or family members. If, however, a spirit is repeatedly called for unimportant reasons, it can unnecessarily retard the growth of the departed soul.

On one occasion when I called this particular soul, he was in class on the Other Side and in order to come talk to us, he had to get permission from a teacher. The teacher told him it was okay for him to be excused from class because the conversations we were going to have with him were actually going to be educational for him and aid in his development. But this is not always the case.

I had another client come to me for a mediumship session in my early days before I knew better. She wanted to talk to a deceased uncle. When I called the uncle in, he was annoyed by her questions. He kept saying, "I left my affairs in order!" The client was able to confirm that he had indeed left his affairs in order—documents, insurance, a will, and so on—but she was convinced that he had never divulged some family secret and she kept asking questions to that effect. The uncle kept telling his niece to talk to her living relatives. When the session was over, the client revealed that although she was asking her uncle questions about other family members, she was not willing to talk to any of them, despite his insistence that she do just that. She had stopped talking to all her family members and had no interest in communicating with them. Instead, she wanted, in effect, to use her uncle to spy on her other relatives. The woman did not have loving words for her uncle. She did not thank him, forgive him, seek to understand him, or listen to any advice he gave her. She only wanted to use him.

I made the mistake, as a medium, of letting an emotionally immature client set the tone of the interaction with her spiritually immature loved one. What they both needed was guidance and assistance in their growth. The deceased uncle did not appear to have done much work since leaving the Earth plane. He was really angry that we were calling on him and asking him questions.

Although he made a little effort to help his niece, he was mostly consumed by his own annoyance at being called down to Earth without good reason. Despite his immaturity he did have a point. Spirits should not be called down to Earth without good reason. If he needed to progress spiritually, coming down to Earth to answer frivolous questions was not going to help him advance, and time spent away from his spirit world lessons and healings could retard his growth. If I had allowed the same client to see me again and again so that she could continue to avoid resolving her own earthly relationships, I would have contributed to the retarding of her spiritual growth as well.

Portals

A *portal* is a doorway connecting one world to another or one dimension to another. Portals can be opened in a variety of ways and can be opened for good or bad reasons. Unfortunately, once a portal is open, the intention of the person who opened it may not be sufficient to limit who or what comes through the portal. Portals can be opened intentionally, and they can also be opened accidentally as the result of certain behaviors.

As a healer I have sometimes worked with a number of angels and archangels (including Michael and Gabriel, well-known in Christianity, as well as Metatron and Chamiel, whose names are only mentioned in ancient Hebrew, Babylonian, and Islamic texts). *Angels* or *devas* are high-level beings who work more closely to Source or God. They are not humans or deceased humans and they have never incarnated on Earth as such. They assist humanity with its development in many ways. Some angels work with plants and animals; others work with humans. Most cultures perceive them as being messengers from God to humans or as high-level beings who help humans in some way. Angels have assisted me my whole life, both as Spirit Teachers and, in recent years, as helpers in my healing practice. When I have someone on my table, I sometimes open up an energy vortex to the angelic realm. By doing this I am able to get assistance from healing angels. I can use the portal to send attached spirits to the light. Angelic orderlies can come through the portal to help me remove stuck energy, negative energy, astral beings, or earthbound spirits from my clients.

Such portals are very important and helpful for healing. But there are other types of portals. A *spirit vortex* allows a psychic access to the Spirit World. Spirits can come in or go out of this type of portal. I can send unwanted spirits to the light through such a portal, but unwanted spirits can also come back through the portal to this dimension if the person opening the portal does not know what they are doing.

Some locations in the world have powerful energy vortexes. Sedona, Arizona, is one such site. In places like Sedona it is possible to move into other dimensions and communicate with angels, extraterrestrials, or interdimensional beings. It is also possible to have powerful out of body experiences in such locations. Throughout the world, lands exist that are designated as sacred. These sacred lands are often home to portals or vortices. In these spaces, fairies, interdimensional beings, or angels can easily enter our world. Because they have natural portals or gateways connecting the land to other realms, sacred lands are often chosen for sacred ceremonies. Ceremonies can be especially powerful in such locations and shamans or medicine people often use such locations to hold important spiritual events that include spirits. These portals can assist a shaman in healing a person, community, or place.

Another type of portal can be opened through spellcasting, filthy magic, or the misuse of sacred plants. These negative portals can become gateways through which negative entities can access our world in order to engage in mischief or seek to take control of humans. I once shared a space with a fellow psychic in New Mexico. One day, she decided to invite some people over to do a "ceremony." This so-called ceremony was essentially just them doing psychedelic herbs without any guidance from a shaman or medicine person. During this event, the group accidentally opened up a negative portal. When drugs and alcohol are used outside of a proper ceremony, they can tear holes in your aura and can attract addicted or mischievous spirits. Their use can also lead to the opening of portals. While you are intoxicated it is easy to become influenced by negative spirits, especially if you have taken no steps to set up sacred space or to protect yourself. Ceremonies without trained ceremonial leaders are risky. If you don't know what you are doing, you may invoke or invite negative entities into a space.

In the case of the portal opened by my fellow psychic, once it was opened, it became a way for nefarious spirits to enter into the space at any time. People who attempted to engage in energy healing in that space were harmed after the portal was created. Some students tried to practice healing in the space after the portal was opened, and as a result, two of the people they were working on got sick and had to be rushed to the hospital. Once a portal is created, the creator may not know how to close it and may not know how to control how it is used, and in this way, a psychic can open a portal that causes others harm. The psychic in New Mexico who inadvertently opened the portal by doing drugs in the space was not powerful enough to close it. She was just beginning on her path and lacked the gifts necessary to close portals.

Supersensory persons must be careful when using controlled substances. They must also be careful when calling spirits or running ceremonies. They must be aware that it is possible to open portals they have no control over. The ethical psychic will avoid taking hallucinogens without the guidance of a medicine person or shaman, and they will not open portals unless they have the training and expertise to close them.

5

HOW TO BECOME AN ETHICAL PSYCHIC

All medicine persons are hollow bones through which Wakan Tanka works.[1]

–FOOLS CROW

A person does not become an ethical psychic by accident. Being a good person with no mal intent is not enough. Doing the work to become an ethical psychic entails certain risks, and practicing without being prepared is enough to create circumstances that can lead to unethical behavior. By choosing, first and foremost, to become an ethical psychic, you are choosing to remain vigilant and to ensure that your work does not harm others. You are also choosing to do the work necessary to avoid the many risks attendant on using your gifts to help others.

CHOOSE TEACHERS CAREFULLY

Some will argue that psychic gifts are bestowed and not learned, that you either have the gift or you do not. The truth is that the very best psychics have undergone extensive training, either formally or informally. Buddhist monks and Hindu yogis meditate for years before they develop *siddhis*.[2] Famous psychics like Sonia Choquette and John Holland studied with a variety of teachers in order to hone their craft.[3] Indigenous healers, shamans, and medicine people throughout the world are expected to apprentice for many years with a master healer before they become good enough to work alone.

Professional psychics must be able to use their gifts on demand. This requires practice, discipline, and good teachers. People who are born with gifts are rarely born with the ability to control their gifts; their gifts are often expressed erratically. Sometimes they know the future. Sometimes they don't. Sometimes they can sense people's thoughts, feelings, or personalities when they meet them, sometimes they cannot. Sometimes they see and hear spirits, sometimes they cannot. If they speak to spirits, the arrival and departure of said spirits is often random and unpredictable.

All psychics can learn to control their gifts; they can practice and train to develop their gifts. With development, they can learn to exercise their gifts in a consistent and reliable way. The more consistent and reliable your gift is, the more people you will be able to help. Therefore, it would behoove all psychics to get as much training as they can to optimize their gifts. Psychic Alexandra Chauran advises the ethical psychic to "be consistently vigilant for more licensing and certification opportunities. . . . Join . . . local chambers of commerce . . . Join professional organizations for the types of . . . work you provide [and] take continuing education."[4]

In addition to continually seeking training to improve the execution and control of your gifts, you should also seek training in related areas such as counseling, coaching, healing, and teaching. A good psychic is not merely gifted but also develops the ability to talk to and guide people, to counsel them, and sometimes to teach them. Rather than learning how to develop all these abilities through self-study and on-the-job training, it is more efficient to benefit from the acquired wisdom of elders, teachers, experts, and wise people. Times change. The demographics of your client pool and their needs will also change over time, and you will need to change with them. Because people's individual problems change over time, you will benefit from learning a wide range of methods to solve these shifting problems.

Seeking out training on a regular basis also helps the psychic to maintain a beginner's mind, a student's mind. A person with a student's mind is humble; she knows how much she doesn't know. The humble psychic is aware that there are others wiser than her. The psychic who has stopped learning has stopped growing. The psychic who forgets how much she doesn't know is in danger of becoming arrogant and willfully ignorant.

Seeking out the advice of elders is something that is encouraged in the Native American and Caribbean healing traditions I was trained in. Traditional Seminole Danny Billy explains, "If you want to be who and what you are, you have to take the time to listen to those elders, so that you can learn those ways."[5] The "Code of Ethics" for Hoodoo rootworkers also emphasizes the importance of continued study. Included in their ethical pledge is the promise: "I will continue to study, apply, and advance my knowledge and understanding of divination, hoodoo, conjure, Rootwork, and related fields. I will ever strive to become more proficient in my practices in order to better serve my clients."[6]

It's essential that you choose your teachers carefully. A psychic without teachers of any kind will often become an unethical psychic. Without a good teacher, a psychic can become lost. Unmoored psychics are dangerous. We all need teachers regardless of how much raw talent we may have. A teacher can guide us, correct us, and give us much-needed feedback. Without a teacher, it is easy to become self-centered, arrogant, or overconfident. The teacher keeps the student's ego in check and keeps them humble and honest. Without a teacher we are less likely to notice our mistakes and thus are more likely to repeat them.

I once knew a woman who had a psychic teacher who claimed to be reading the Akashic Records. Although the teacher may indeed have been accessing materials from the soul library, it was clear that not all of her readings came from a higher source. She mixed her own opinions in with reports from the Records. On the surface, this appeared to be a simple case of insufficient psychic development. Beginning students are often guilty of making this mistake because they are unsure of when they are receiving information and when they are making it up. They become confused. Learning how to distinguish personal beliefs from psychic information is key to developing your psychic gifts. But in the case of this "teacher," it wasn't confusion—it was deception. She used the authority of the Records to manipulate her clients and students, and it was no surprise when, at a certain point, one of her students began to employ the same deceitful practices. The student admitted that she had once purposely shaken her body as if in a trance and exclaimed to her lover that "they" (spirits or guides) were telling her to tell her something. Later, after she became aware of the unethical nature of doing such work, she confided that she had told her lover this for her own purposes and that there were no spirits and no trance, and it had all been a ruse. In retrospect, it was not surprising that this student would follow in the footsteps of her teacher. Students tend to do that. The unethical teacher taught the student how to become an unethical psychic. As this example demonstrates, extreme care must be taken in choosing a teacher lest the psychic finds herself learning the wrong lessons, modeling herself after the wrong expert, or making the same mistakes again and again, without correction.

Make sure to avoid teachers who view themselves as gurus who cannot be questioned. Psychics who develop their gifts in the context of an authoritarian community may find themselves learning how to be arrogant and how to use their gifts to control others.

CHOOSE COLLEAGUES CAREFULLY

Although it is not as important as choosing teachers, choosing colleagues carefully is still necessary to avoid getting yourself involved in the unethical practices of others. If you share a space or go into business with a fellow psychic or healer, or if you use the services of a professional in another field (like sales or marketing) and that person is not ethical, you may find yourself becoming an accessory to a harm imposed on a client. If your clients trust you, they may trust your colleagues by association.

I once worked at a large psychic shop where I discovered the owners were employing magick and Brujeria to get clients to return to their shop and buy more products. I was not using magick and I was helping clients, but at a certain point, I had to accept the fact that by working there, I was providing the shop with legitimacy. Clients might rightfully assume that an honest psychic would not work for dishonest people. Although I could have simply focused on my own behavior and assured myself that as long as I was treating my clients well I had nothing to worry about, I decided it was best to no longer be associated with them. I could have chosen to take responsibility only for my own actions and nobody else's, but to do so would have made me indirectly complicit in their deceit.

EXAMINE YOUR MOTIVES

Not everyone with psychic gifts decides to use them, and even fewer decide to hang a shingle and work in some capacity as a professional psychic, medium, or healer. If you are among the few who have decided to use your gifts in a professional capacity, it will be important to ask yourself some questions:

* Are you seeking power over people or circumstances?
* Are you seeking money or fame?
* Are you trying to find a way to quit a job you hate?

* Are you trying to impress someone or intimidate someone?

* Are you motivated to do psychic work for reasons not related to service?

Certain motivations can create conflicts of interest that could negatively impact your clients. When your motivation is service, placing the welfare of the client first follows naturally from your purpose; whereas if you are motivated by financial gain, you may find it difficult to decide what to do when you have to make a decision that requires sacrificing income in order to help your client. If your motivation is to impress someone or please someone, there are many clients who will come to you again and again because you tell them what they want to hear. You can make good money reading for wealthy clients who are willing to pay someone to confirm their beliefs and validate their decisions. Doing this work will not help your clients, however. Telling the client what they don't want to hear can be costly for you as well. If finances are your primary motivation, you may have a hard time being honest with such clients.

When your motivation is unclear, you set yourself up to disregard the risks already discussed. For example, emotional dependency is not recognized as a problem for the psychic whose primary motivation is financial. They may tend to dismiss the problem of client dependency as "not my problem." They may explain it away, saying the client is an adult and must make their own decisions about how often they see the psychic and how much they want to rely on the psychic to the exclusion of other forms of emotional support. If the psychic is motivated by fame or status, they may resort to gimmicks or ploys to impress their clients and the community in order to generate press coverage.

DO THE EMOTIONAL WORK

There is no correlation between psychic gifts and spiritual evolution. A spiritually backward person can be highly gifted in certain supersensory areas. Similarly, there is no correlation between psychic gifts and emotional maturity. A person can be a gifted psychic without having any understanding of their own emotions, much less those of their clients. Emotionally immature people can engage in all kinds of inappropriate and unprofessional behavior because they have not done their own internal work.

We all have emotional wounds from childhood or adulthood—disappointments, heartaches, or instances of trauma and oppression. Although some of us have had more challenges than others, everyone has had to deal with emotional upsets in their life, and these upsets may have caused stagnation or led to poor emotional habits. At some point we all need to process our emotional wounds and heal them. If we do not, those unresolved emotions will become a filter through which we access our gifts and negatively impact our readings.

I remember being a student in mediumship class and noticing that certain novices tended to give the same readings again and again as a result of unprocessed emotional wounds. If, for example, a medium had experienced a bad relationship with her father, whenever she would bring through someone's father, she would describe the spirit as having the same negative attributes her father had. Similarly, when a psychic had experienced bad relationships in the past and had failed to process emotions related to those relationships, he projected his feelings onto clients who resembled those people. This resulted in psychics making judgment calls instead of giving readings.

For example, if you are an angry person you may focus on anger in your clients. If you have a victim consciousness, you may pick up attachments from your clients, or you may have a large number of clients with a victim consciousness who are unwilling to change and who are not open to what you tell them. Like attracts like and your emotional wounds will attract people to you with the same wounds. If you have not done the internal work to heal your emotional and spiritual wounds, you will be uniquely unsuited to helping people with theirs.

It is important for anyone going into a supersensory profession to spend serious time and energy doing the emotional work. Read self-help books, go to seminars, see a therapist, or join a support group— but become self-aware. A psychic who is not self-aware is at greater risk of engaging in unethical behaviors. She may find herself getting involved in unhealthy emotional relationships with her clients or she may use her gifts to have an unfair advantage in her intimate relationships. She may also engage in armchair psychology, advising her clients on how to handle emotional relationships from a place of ignorance.

Unprocessed emotions can also lead to inappropriate encounters on the astral plane. Often, when we have intense emotions that we have not thoroughly processed on the Earth plane, we visit the astral plane at night to work through them there. This can be problematic if those visits involve other people. A jilted lover can "stalk" his ex on the astral plane, trying to initiate affective, romantic, or sexual relations with the ex energetically. The victim of such visits may experience these visits as intense dreams or nightmares. Although some people meet on the astral plane through mutual consent, if one partner is more gifted than the other, there is a power imbalance that can allow one person to overpower another. Similarly, if one person is especially vulnerable, he may be easy to influence on the astral plane.

It's not enough for a psychic to become trained in how to consciously visit different planes, how to go out of body, or how to remember one's dreams. If the gifted person has not dealt with their emotional wounds, they will find themselves repeatedly drawn to the astral plane. On the Earth plane, a psychic who has low self-esteem may tend to become arrogant in an attempt to prove to everyone that they are worthy of esteem. They may overcompensate by insisting that their readings are always 100 percent accurate when they are not. A psychic who was raised in an alcoholic or addictive environment may become a codependent who feels the need to take care of her clients. This can result in unhealthy boundaries between psychic and client. A psychic who was abused or mistreated repeatedly as a child or as an adult may come to think of people as inherently bad and untrustworthy and the world as unfair. They can then justify behaving in excessively self-serving ways and exploit others because they were exploited.

Emotional wounds can also impair a psychic's ability to receive information clearly. Trauma, assumptions, and bias can all mar a psychic's ability to get accurate information about clients belonging to certain demographics. Thus, for example, a psychic who has been disrespected by a number of men in their life may come to hold certain beliefs about all men, and these generalizations can cause them to misinterpret information they receive from or about a particular man. Similarly, a psychic who was raised in a repressive religious or cultural environment may develop strong negative generalized views about religion, spirituality, or certain cultures, and these prejudices may cause them to misrepresent information they intuitively receive related to those contexts. Instead of allowing unprocessed emotional wounds to limit their ability to access and deliver information to the client, the ethical psychic would do well to do the work of processing and healing the emotional wounds related to those contexts.

One effective way to address unprocessed emotions is to work with a therapist, coach, or spiritual counselor. Meditation is also quite helpful. A daily practice of meditation can improve both emotional and physical health. At the very least, you should meditate once per day, and ideally, you should meditate before and after a long or difficult reading or healing session. It is easy to meditate with all of the phone apps now available and all of the YouTube meditation videos out there. Mediation allows you to cleanse your own energy and to better connect to your client's energy; it will also help you to connect directly with high-vibration source energy, Higher Self, or guides. Meditation also has numerous scientifically verified benefits for reducing stress, improving health, increasing mental clarity, and increasing life span.[7] Meditation will help you to discard the emotional and ener-getic debris you have accumulated in the course of your day or from your other clients. It will help you to become a clear channel.

Famed mystic and founder of Questhaven Retreat Flower Newhouse explains that

> *Daily meditation is as essential as nourishing food. Regularity in the practice brings us a sense of an ever-widening consciousness... The effort necessary to inner sight is not a matter of strength or determination, but rather of character development and a positive receptivity. These qualifications unfold through meditation and an exercise of the inner faculties in us.*[8]

Getting in the habit of taking a daily emotional inventory is as important as meditating daily for an ethical psychic. Doing an inventory will help you to become more emotionally aware. Make it a habit to ask yourself, "What am I feeling and why? What is my emotional state at this time, and can I adjust it in order to be a hollow bone (defined momentarily) for this reading?" You should be aware of what you are feeling and be able to distinguish your emotions from those you might pick up through clairsentience. Clairsentient feelings provide important information that you can use in a client session. If you are not aware of your own emotions, you will not be able to use the clairsentient information you receive. Doing a daily emotional inventory also helps prevent you from projecting your own emotional issues onto your client. When you are emotionally overwrought, you should take a break from working with clients.

DEDICATE YOURSELF TO
BECOMING A HOLLOW BONE

The Sioux Holy man Black Elk once said, "I cured with the power that came through me. Of course, it was not I who cured. It was the power from the outer world and the visions and ceremonies had only made me like a hole through which the power could come to the two-leggeds."⁹ Sioux medicine man Fools Crow, ceremonial chief of the Teton Sioux, agreed with Black Elk in his description of healing, adding that it is best to think of medicine people as "little hollow bones."¹⁰ When the psychic-healer is a *hollow bone*, the energy, the healing, the information, flows *through* them, not from them. Fools Crow further explains that "medicine and holy people work the hardest to become clean. The cleaner the bone, the more water you can pour through it and the faster it will run. It is this way with us and power, and the holy person is the one who becomes the cleanest of all."¹¹

Psychics who view themselves and their gift as something that works through them, rather than by them are less likely to misuse their gift. A hollow bone psychic-healer knows that she is merely the vehicle through which her gift is delivered to the people who need it. As a hollow bone, the healer's job is to get out of the way and let Spirit/Prana/The Power work. Well-known twentieth century medical intuitive and healer Henry Rucker, who first introduced Norman Shealy to the field of medical intuition and later served as the pastoral counselor at the Shealy Institute for Pain and Health Rehabilitation for fifteen years, explains his role as a hollow bone thus: "I do not feel basically that I am the one who does the healing. I can't tell you why but maybe God chose me as one of the channels."¹²

When you dedicate yourself to becoming a hollow bone, you dedicate yourself to a vigilant program of self-cleansing, purification, and humility. Being a hollow bone means being pure and as clean as possible so that the information can flow through you without getting stuck on you. One of the greatest obstacles to becoming a consistently accurate psychic is the ego. When we get in the way—when we try to take charge of deciding what the information we get *should* mean, we risk corrupting and misinterpreting the information. We become dirty bones—clogged with opinions, assumptions, judgments, and prejudices. We end up filtering the information we get through who we are and what we believe. Our moods and individual biases interfere with the information we receive, thus rendering our readings inaccurate, inconsistent, or incomplete. Medium Peter Brown explains, "The channel through which the information comes has to be reconstructed, has to lose opinions, instead of being opinionated. One has to be willing to lose the ego."[13]

The ego likes to be right. It is prideful and boastful and cares too much about what others think. The ego competes and judges and challenges. That said, the ego is essential for survival, and in many contexts, it is an extremely important and central aspect of ourselves. However, the ego is not responsible for the information we receive psychically. When the ego is not kept in check, it can obstruct our ability to be hollow bones, to receive intuitive information clearly, and to deliver it in an unbiased way. The ego, when unchecked, can cause us to be more concerned with being right than with being accurate or helpful. It can tempt us into false beliefs like "I am always right," "My predictions always come true." "My hunches about people are always correct." "I am a better psychic than most." Such beliefs hinder your growth as a psychic and can impede your ability to help others. The unchecked ego can also get in the way of an objective evaluation of the facts. It can hamper a psychic's ability to hear unfavorable feedback. The unchecked ego can prevent a psychic from receiving psychic messages that conflict with their beliefs or judgments. If the psychic is more concerned with being right than with delivering the information received, they can do real damage to the client.

Some people believe that psychic gifts are a matter of power and that the more power you have, the greater a psychic you will be. But power without ethics is dangerous and those who focus on power will be limited in the gifts they can develop. The ego, when unchecked, limits our receptivity to Spirit and thus stunts our growth as psychics. The ethical psychic is not overly concerned with being right. She is concerned with being helpful.

World-renowned psychic Sonia Choquette, in her memoir *Diary of a Psychic*, recounts what her teacher, Charlie, taught her about the ego:

Charlie was absolutely adamant that I understand why I was psychic and that I use my channel for the correct reasons. "You are not an entertainer," he scolded, "and to entertain others with your gifts solely as a means of being the center of attention is a gross violation of your talent, and you will suffer for it." Charlie constantly warned me, "Your gifts are to serve spirit and God, and not ever, ever your personal ego."[14]

Being a hollow bone means letting the information flow unimpeded; allowing the images, words, and feelings to come; and delivering them without censorship, editing, or distortion—all while banishing fear, doubt, and worry about the content of the material that comes. As a hollow bone you are not the architect nor the originator of the information you receive; you are merely the messenger. As the messenger, you have no justification for becoming arrogant or boastful about your ability. A messenger can claim no glory with regard to the context of the message for it does not originate with them. Psychics who dedicate themselves to becoming hollow bones will do everything they can to keep the message pure by keeping themselves pure. They will engage in rituals of physical, emotional, and spiritual purification on a regular basis and will resist the temptation of egoism. The ethical psychic strives always to be a hollow bone, knowing that the surrender of the ego will increase their ability to help and never hurt their clients.

In the words of the Her Majesty Dowoti Désir, Queen Mother and Grand Vodun Priestess, "As priests we come to understand we are in the world to be thoughtfully tutored by Spirit and to uphold our sacraments through a predetermined relationship to the ancestors, God, and the world."[15]

LIVE A BALANCED LIFE

Living a balanced life is important for everyone, but it is especially important for the ethical psychic. A balanced life includes work and play, seriousness and silliness, time with family, and time with friends or romantic partners. In a balanced life, all of a person's needs can be met because time spent on various activities is in proportion to a person's needs. A balanced life satisfies the needs of the physical, emotional, and spiritual aspects of humanity. A life in which excessive attention is given to only the emotional, the mental, the physical, or the spiritual aspects is an unbalanced, disharmonious life.

When a healer fails to get all his needs met in a healthy way, he is more susceptible to engaging in behaviors that are potentially injurious to his clients and himself. If, for example, a psychic fails to devote time and space to nurturing affective and sexual relationships with people, he may find himself developing such relationships with his clients. If he is lonely and lacking in friends, he might befriend or date his clients and thus be at risk of engaging in a misuse of sexual energy. If the psychic is not satisfying his normal human needs outside of his work, he may satisfy them within his client relationships.

Everyone needs emotional support, camaraderie, praise, love, affection, romance. Everyone needs someone who listens to them, who appreciates, admires, and respects them, and who makes them feel important and needed. If you lack these things in your personal life, the attention of a client can tempt you to get your needs met by that person. A false and rapid intimacy can arise in the context of any sort of healing—whether psychic or energetic. The prudent psychic will avoid misinterpreting this intimacy as something other than a byproduct of this powerful exchange of energy.

Although the client may not be able to distinguish between strong energetic attraction and sexual attraction, the psychic should know better. But even psychics who "know better" may find themselves tempted to engage in inappropriate dual relationships if their needs are not being met in other aspects of their life. Living an unbalanced life not only harms the psychic but it also has the potential to harm the clients.

6

FREQUENTLY ASKED QUESTIONS

As a teacher of numerous psychic and healing modalities, I get a lot of questions from my students about the dos and don'ts of psychic work, the journey of the soul, and the implications of giving certain kinds of readings. This chapter answers many of the questions that I routinely get asked in the instructional setting. I also used to run a Transformation and Wellness (Psychic and Healing) Faire in which I decided to set only one ground rule: Don't share the Three Ds with your clients in a fifteen-minute session. This ground rule sparked conversations in a circle of practicing psychics, and in this chapter, I address some of the questions that came up in that setting.

QUESTION # 1: THE THREE DS—IS IT OKAY TO TELL MY CLIENT THAT THEY ARE DYING, THAT THEY HAVE A DEADLY DISEASE, OR THAT THEY ARE ABOUT TO GET DIVORCED?

Some psychics believe you should deliver whatever information you get and that you should answer all questions directly and truthfully. The ethical psychic will ask whether the bold truth is going to be helpful and healing. Are you giving them the bad news because your ego needs to be right, to make an accurate prediction, or for the sake of the drama? The ethical psychic only tells their client bad news if they believe it is what their client needs to hear in order to effect a positive transformation in their life.

Before sharing one of the three Ds, your motive must be pure. There is danger entailed in making predictions. Care must be taken because such predictions can become self-fulfilling prophecies, and in this way, you could be guilty of perverting the will of your client. To avoid doing so, a psychic should choose language carefully and remind the client that the future is not set—that they have the power to control their own destiny. For example, a psychic might say to a client, "If you continue on your current path, it will end in divorce." Such a statement allows a client to make changes and avert the predicted fate. Similarly, with a life-threatening disease, you might tell them that if they do not make drastic changes in their life, they will develop the disease.

Before sharing three D information, make sure the client can handle it. It is important for the psychic to tune in to the client to access what they need to hear and how they need to hear it.

Death is its own special case. When it comes to predicting death, it is vital that the psychic takes the attitude of the client and the environment or culture she lives in into account. In a country like the US, pervaded by a nearly universal fear of death, predictions of death can cause great suffering, whereas in a society that accepts death as a natural part of life, predictions of death might allow the client and their family to make preparations. Consider the context before predicting possible death for a client.

I once had a client, in his eighties, in whom I discovered a large, inoperable blood clot in the center of his brain (this clot was later confirmed by an MRI scan). I saw that he was going to die and there was no fix for this. When I tuned in to him, I saw, too, that he was ready to die. He was satisfied with his life and was ready to move on.

If I had been working directly with him, I could have assured him that it was okay to leave. But his granddaughter had ordered and paid for the scan I was conducting, and although I had gotten verbal consent from the man to run the scan, he had requested that I send the scan report to his granddaughter. This meant the granddaughter would also be reading the scan report, so I had to take her feelings into account.

The granddaughter was not ready to lose her grandfather, so I had to be careful in how I worded everything. I told them the clot was inoperable (later confirmed by his doctor). I suggested some natural remedies to help with brain function and to help absorb some of the blood that was pooling in the brain and made suggestions for treatment that would assist him with the headaches and other symptoms. In other words, I offered a treatment plan for *palliative* care not *curing* care. In my report, I talked about all the grandfather had accomplished in his life and suggested that the family take two actions: 1) organize a large family gathering to celebrate his life and 2) embark on an oral history of his life. In effect, I told the grandfather and granddaughter to get their affairs in order.

When it comes to predictions of death, I find that giving advice along the lines of 1) get your affairs in order/tie up loose ends; 2) live life as if today is your last; or 3) reflect on your life/do a retrospective on your accomplishments to be the most helpful. Actually uttering the statement "You are going to die soon" isn't always necessary or helpful.

However, sometimes people *do* need to be told they are dying because sometimes this is the best medicine. Sometimes they need someone to tell them that it is okay to leave. Sometimes they need to know so they can take some action. Sometimes telling them can help them to make choices about treatment options. But most people in the West cannot handle being told they are going to die, and I suggest that ethical psychics avoid predicting death unless there is some good that will come from it.

QUESTION #2: DOES KARMA EXIST AND DOES THAT MEAN EVERYONE GETS THEIR JUST DESERTS?

Karma, as a concept, is widely misunderstood, and as a result, its effects are often misinterpreted. In particular, people can misapply the notion of karmic debts and rewards to evade responsibility for their actions. For example, a person born with a privileged body or lifestyle (as defined by their societies where hierarchies of gender, race, religion, caste, class, and able-bodiedness exist) will often attribute their privileges to acquiring a body gifted to them to reward them for past lives well-lived. Such persons may feel comfortable turning a blind eye to the suffering of those persons born into oppressed bodies with the self-assurance that these people deserved their fate because of past-life misdeeds or accrued karmic debts.

Karma is not a system of rewards and punishments. Souls are not condemned to lives of oppression because they have lived immoral lives in the past. Neither are the most highly evolved souls gifted with lives of privilege or luxury. Lives that are free of obstacles and challenges—whether because of privilege or because of what is perceived as good luck—are not evidence that a soul has evolved or is blameless. Rather, such lives often indicate that the soul chose not to work hard this time around. Challenges, obstacles, and oppression are all opportunities for soul growth. Sometimes souls are unwilling to work on their growth; other times they are tired and decide to experience a *vacation life* of ease.[1] If the ease that the soul experiences is the direct result of hierarchies of privilege and oppression, the soul risks incurring additional karma in that lifetime. For example, if a soul incarnates as a rich white male and goes on to mistreat servants, disrespect women, or become a racist, he will incur karma. Privilege makes life easier, but it is riskier where incurring karma is concerned.

Karma is balance. When souls perpetuate harm against other souls, they are given the opportunity to balance that harm in various ways. For example, I once had a client who was a mixed-race African American child adopted by white parents. In a previous incarnation, the mixed boy had been a Black man enslaved by whites in the United States. As an enslaved man he had organized a slave revolt but had been caught and lynched. The man who caught and killed him was his adoptive father in this lifetime. The woman who was his current mother had attended the lynching in the past life as a wealthy white woman spectator. She had not killed him, but she had failed to speak out against his murder even though she knew it was wrong. In that life she had the status and power to interfere and possibly prevent his death if she had spoken out.

In this life, these two souls—the murderer and the woman who was complicit—pledged to take care of the soul they had killed in the previous life. Karma did not require these souls to be punished, but karma impelled them to seek out an opportunity to play a different role, and to have a different relationship with the soul who had been unjustly murdered as an enslaved man. Being the parents of this soul was not a punishment, but it was an opportunity to repair the damage they had done in the previous incarnation and to experience a different type of relationship with that soul.

Karma is often about balancing out life choices and providing a group of souls with opportunities to grow. Souls who have had numerous lifetimes as one gender are then given the opportunity to incarnate as another gender in order to balance out the souls' experience. A soul who has experienced wealth will choose lives of poverty or a soul who has enjoyed a vigorous body will choose a life of disability or poor health to learn the lessons that such lives provide. Sometimes souls choose to try to rectify their perceived past-life mistakes by entering into soul contracts with souls they have harmed in past lives. A soul can seek to rectify past wrongs with current good acts, or they can change places with the other soul in order to learn compassion. Thus, a soul who in their last life was bedridden and dependent upon relatives for care might choose in this lifetime to care for a disabled family member who was the able-bodied caretaker in the last life. In these ways, both souls have a more well-rounded experience of human life. In addition, both souls can learn compassion by seeing a situation from both sides.

Misunderstanding the nature of karma can lead to a relegation of responsibility. If you believe that all things will be balanced out by karma, you may then decide that community injustices perpetuated against others are of no earthly consequence. It is important for the psychic-healer, who deals with past lives, to understand what karma is and is not in order to avoid misinterpreting the meaning of a past life for a client. If clients use karma as an excuse not to take responsibility for their actions in this life, they do injury to themselves and others.

What I have often seen with my clients is that they have chosen to incarnate on both sides of a conflict or struggle for karmic reasons. Thus, a soul will incarnate as a member of an oppressive ruling family in one life and as an oppressed peasant whose life is controlled by a ruling family in another. Or else a soul will live one life as a Native American and another life as a white settler or cowboy. I have seen souls who incarnated as Jewish victims of the holocaust and then as Nazi sympathizers, as colonizers and then as colonized people, as women oppressed by men and as men who oppress women. What I have not seen is souls being punished in one life for what they did in a previous life. Nor is it the case that everyone experiences both sides of every conflict. Choosing lives is like choosing courses in college. Not everyone chooses the hardest courses. Some people prefer to skate through school by choosing the easiest classes they can find, hoping to graduate after putting in the least amount of work. Similarly, some souls take on difficult lives as oppressed people and some do not. The souls who take on the oppressed lives are often the more advanced, more courageous souls—the souls most interested in evolving quickly.[2]

QUESTION #3: IS IT OKAY TO ANSWER QUESTIONS ABOUT PEOPLE WHO ARE NOT PRESENT AT THE READING?

Most people who hire private detectives do not do so to catch crooks or locate lost items or missing children. They do so to catch cheating spouses. Some people find it cheaper and more expedient to consult a psychic to spy on their family members. An ethical psychic should always consider issues of privacy as well as possible consequences of revealing secrets, affairs, and intrigues to their clients.

If a client comes and asks for a reading, you have that person's permission to snoop around in *their* aura, *their* energy bodies, *their* past lives, and so on, but that does not mean you have permission to snoop into the affairs of everyone they know. Thus, when a client comes to me asking about their spouse or lover or child, I provide information that is relevant to the client and the relationship with the person in question. When they start asking me about things that they want to know about others out of pure nosiness, I do not assist them. For example, if a client needs to know if their spouse is lying to them, cheating on them, engaged in illegal activity, or planning to harm them, I answer their questions as long as the information will help them and help their relationship. But if a client comes to me and asks questions about other people that have nothing to do with them or asks questions about people they are not in relationships with, I do not assist them.

When psychics get involved in the relationships of their clients, they risk damaging those relationships. Care must be taken in handling such clients. One particular kind of client is the *helicopter parent*, a parent who is overly involved in their child's life. Even after their children are grown, these parents remain convinced that they must know everything about their child's life. While it is understandable that parents whose children refuse to talk to them might feel they need to consult a psychic to obtain news of their absent offspring, sometimes clients can request too much information. It is better to provide the parent with information about the child that might increase their understanding. Such improved understanding could help them repair the fractured or absent connection between parent and child. The danger comes when the parent substitutes psychic spying for an actual connection to and reconciliation with the prodigal child.

QUESTION #4: WHEN DO I GIVE A REFUND?

It depends on the situation. We all have off days as psychics, and it is important to be self-aware enough to know when you are having a bad day. If the reading is not going well and the information is not coming as smoothly as usual, why not just offer the client a refund before they ask? They may refuse the refund and insist that you continue and give it your best shot. If they are not happy with the reading thus far, however, if you offer a refund, they can walk away happy, and you can avoid wasting your time by continuing a reading that is unlikely to be one of your best.

On the other hand, if your reading is going well but the client does not like what you are telling them and they demand a refund simply because they didn't want to hear that Mr. X is Mr. Wrong, then they do not deserve a refund. But your client may not see it this way. So how do you protect yourself from such clients? And how do you ensure that the clients who deserve refunds get them? Here are a few things you can do:

1. Communicate clearly to the client upfront about exactly what you do and what you don't do. Sometimes clients are disappointed because they were expecting you to deliver more than you could or were expecting you to work in ways that you don't. Be very clear in your advertising about what you do. If necessary, ask some clarifying questions or make some service-defining statements at the outset of the session so you and the client are on the same page. You can

also have clients sign a waiver in which you spell out what you do.

2. Publish a refund policy up front that indicates under what conditions you will issue a refund, that you have a policy of no refunds, or that you are able to issue partial refunds. Whatever your policy is, publish it ahead of time and make sure the client agrees to it before you begin the reading.

3. Use your intuition to weed out potential clients who are scam artists who habitually try to get services for free. These people exist. If you get a bad vibe from a potential client, you are better off just politely declining to book them. If their focus is the hustle, they are unlikely to benefit from what you have to tell them anyway. This means turning some clients away. It may look like you are losing money, but in the long run, turning away such clients will save you money and could save your reputation.

Sometimes you will have to refund a client who does not deserve a refund. Keep in mind that in this era of online reviews, customers use and abuse review platforms to have leverage over businesses with whom they are unhappy. If a customer demands a refund and you refuse to grant it, they may retaliate with a bad review that hurts the reputation of your business. Sometimes a refund is a fee you pay for making a bad choice of client. Consider it tuition for a lesson well learned and move on. Also keep in mind that clients who ask for refunds are sometimes doing so because they cannot handle what you have told them in the session. Refusing to pay for a session may be their way of trying to delegitimize the information in their mind. They may be trying to initiate a fight with you so that they can convince themselves that you are no good. Let them win the money battle. What you have told them might sink in at a later date. Rest in your knowledge that you have delivered a valuable service to them whether or not they are ready to receive it at this time.

The ethical psychic views refund requests as a part of her training. By paying attention to who asks for refunds and when, by looking for patterns, and by using these patterns, the psychic can become more self-aware about her accuracy rates, can improve her delivery, and can learn how to weed out dishonest clients.

QUESTION #5: ARE THERE SOME CLIENTS I SHOULD NOT WORK WITH?

The ethical psychic wants to help and never harm her clients. Sometimes refusing to work with a client is the best way to help them. It is not a good idea to work with clients who have proven themselves to be overly dependent, who cannot afford the sessions, who are not being helped by the sessions, who are not ethically prepared to use the information, or who are in need of other services (such as medical treatment or psychological counseling) and are using psychic sessions as a way to avoid addressing their problems.

Do not see a client who is demonstrating dependency. If a client is prone to obsession, is seeking a guru, or has a hard time making decisions for himself, it may be best to limit or end your interaction with such a client. (See "Unethical Risk #2: Client Dependency" in Chapter 2 for more on codependency.) Excessively needy clients don't actually need you; they need to learn how to trust themselves. If you can help them to trust themselves more, then you should continue to help them. If, however, a client is just becoming more dependent upon you over time, you should consider no longer seeing them. The ethical psychic does not sacrifice the well-being of her client in order to make money. Clients grow at different rates, and although some clients need one session to kick start a transformation in their lives, others need more time and more assistance.

When your client becomes dependent upon you, they can no longer benefit from sessions. The purpose of the psychic-healer is to assist the client in solving problems and in healing and transforming their life. An addicted client is attempting to give away their power and has abdicated responsibility for their own life. If your client has become needy and dependent, that means that the help you have given them has failed to help them learn how to help themselves. Your services have not empowered them, and this is not good.

Although a client may return to you repeatedly, they should not come back in a state of desperation. They should show some evidence of growth over time. As you continue to work with them, you should be working on new issues and new problems after the original problems are solved. You should look for evidence that the client is applying the advice you are giving them to their life and that their life is improving. They should be happier and more peaceful over time as a result of working with you. They should not be coming to see you about the same problem for months without making any progress.

If a client shows signs of dependency, the ethical psychic should place limits on how frequently she will book sessions with that client. The psychic should insist that the client take a break or that a certain amount of time passes between sessions. Ethical psychics will also set clear boundaries regarding communication with the client and do not allow their clients to call them at all hours of the day and night. The ethical psychic will not allow herself to become an on-call crisis psychic hotline as this is unlikely to empower her client.

It is also not a good idea to work with clients who are interested in casting spells on other people, for the purpose of manipulating or overpowering other people. Even if you are not providing a spellcasting service for them directly, if you know they are motivated in this way, you must recognize that any information you give them can aid them in their nefarious efforts. If they do not have the ethical backbone to use the information you give them wisely, do not give it to them. Make sure your client is ready for the information you have for them before you give it to them.

Do not see a client who cannot afford you if you cannot adjust your price to something they can afford. When possible, an ethical psychic should pay attention to the financial distress of their clients. If a client is repeatedly coming to a psychic for help with financial woes and the psychic consultation fees are steep, the psychic may need to offer the client one discounted or free session or discourage the client from booking more consultations. Although a client's financial choices are their own and the psychic is not responsible for these choices, it is incumbent upon the psychic not to knowingly aggravate a bad situation by taking money from a financially desperate client. If the purpose of the consultation is to improve their finances but the consultations are not helping with that, the sessions should be discontinued. A psychic who knowingly encourages a financially strapped client to buy expensive consultations is contributing to the client's financial woes.

Do not see a client who either doesn't want help or is not being helped by you. Sometimes a client will go from psychic to psychic asking the same question. There is nothing wrong with this; it is like collecting data. But when a client asks the same psychic the same question over and over, this is a problem. Either the client is not listening to the answers he is receiving, the answers the psychic is providing are not helpful, or the client is only interested in one answer and will keep asking until he gets it. In any of these cases, the psychic has no reason to continue to see the client and take his money. Whether the fault lies with the psychic for providing inadequate information or with the client who has chosen not to listen to the information the psychic offered, the result is the same: the consultations are providing neither a transformation nor a healing, and thus they should stop.

Another category of client that the psychic should be wary of working with is the client who has a serious medical or mental health condition. If a client is very sick, it will be important for the psychic to urge the client to get medical care. The psychic must make it clear that the information she provides is no substitute for medical care. If the client is dealing with a life-threatening ailment, the psychic may choose not to work with them because anything the psychic says about the illness could have a far-reaching impact on the welfare of the client. An ethical psychic should also avoid working with a suicidal client as one wrong word could send such a person over the edge. The psychic should suggest that such a client seek emergency counseling and assist them in locating resources if necessary rather than giving them a reading. It is also a good idea to avoid working with clients who have untreated or poorly treated mental illness because a reading could cause injury to the client, the psychic, or someone else if the client is unstable.

Finally, it is always best to be cautious with minors; if a psychic is going to see a child, they should do so only with the consent of the parent. For very young children, the parent should be present for the reading, and for older children, such as teenagers, the psychic should require that the reading be recorded for the parents. Children should not be seen in private without a parent either in the room or nearby, and the psychic must be careful not to touch or hug the child without the presence and permission of the parent. Care must be taken with language as well. Children are sensitive beings and the language you use with an adult cannot be used with a child. If the psychic has no experience with or training on how to interact with children, she should avoid working with this client pool. Psychics should be especially careful when predicting the future for children because they are so impressionable. The psychic must know how *not* to answer certain questions that a child might ask because the child may not be mature enough to handle the answer. It is a good idea for the psychic to discuss questions with the parent before the session begins. Keep the reading light and fun when working with children and always include their parents in every aspect of the work.

If you are unsure about how to talk to a young child you can read the child without them being present. The parent then can choose how much of the reading to share with the child. When working with older teens who are mature, however, the teens must be given the information directly. If the teen is mature, I will sometimes ask the parent if the teen can have a private session while the parent stays outside and I record the session for the parent. If a psychic wants to see a child under eighteen without having a parent present or without recording the session, the parent will need to sign a waiver so that the psychic is not held liable for anything the teen fails to disclose to the parent. By law, teachers and therapists are required to report to officials when a child reports child abuse or is considering suicide. Although psychics are not bound by the same laws, it is advisable for them to follow the same rules when it comes to protecting children from harm. If a child were to indicate to me in a session that they were being harmed by their parent, or if my reading of them revealed this to be the case, I would not allow the parent access to the recording and I would seek to assist the child in getting help instead. Teenagers are clever; although you may tell them to record a session, if they are determined that their parents not hear it, they will erase it or claim their phone was malfunctioning. The psychic is only responsible for doing everything in their power to keep the child safe.

QUESTION #6: IS IT OKAY TO
READ FOR FAMILY MEMBERS?

Because we are emotionally invested in the answers we get for family and close friends, such readings are more challenging. Family members also tend to be our greatest critics, so their expectations might be high or impossible to satisfy. Just because family is difficult to read for doesn't mean doing so is unethical. However, when working with family members, we must keep in mind the same precautions we have with other clients.

You may be tempted to be more casual, less rigorous, and less serious about the work you do for family. Family may also expect you to help them for free, they may expect you to work at inappropriate times and places, and they may be too demanding, thus jeopardizing your ability to do your best work. Try, as much as possible, to treat family the way you treat other clients. Set limits with them and explain to them that there are conditions you require to do your best work. Be vigilant in doing your emotional inventory before working with family and be ready to say no to certain readings if you feel too attached to the outcome.

QUESTION #7: IS IT OKAY TO DATE MY CLIENT IF WE ARE BOTH CONSENTING ADULTS?

Some people will say that as long as the people engaged in a romantic or sexual liaison are consenting adults there is no harm in connecting. The problem with using this logic to evaluate relationships between clients and psychics revolves around how we define *consent*. Because psychics are in a power position and can use their psychic power to manipulate others, discussions of consent must include energetic consent. The power dynamic between two people at two different levels of development can manifest as an energetic inequality. When such inequality exists, the psychic can manipulate the client energetically in order to obtain their consent in the physical realm. The psychic can do this intentionally or unintentionally. If the client is less psychically developed than the psychic, they may not be aware of these energetic manipulations and may consent without knowing they are being energetically seduced. When one person is more psychically gifted than another, and when the more psychically gifted one uses their gifts to get what they want from someone who is not as powerful, there is no consent. To consent, you must *know* you are consenting and you must have the option to choose not to.

QUESTION #8: SHOULD I CUT
MY CLIENT'S CORDS?

Often a psychic-healer will have clients coming to her who are in dysfunctional, chaotic, unhealthy, or even dangerous relationships. For the healer who knows how to do it, it is tempting to cut cords linking the client to these unhealthy relationships, especially if those relationships are impeding the client's growth. But a healer must take every precaution before cutting cords.

First, the healer must ask the client's permission before cutting any cords. The healer should not assume that, just because the relationships are toxic, the client wants the connections to these people to be severed. In the same way that many people partake of substances like cigarettes, alcohol, and sugar, despite knowing such substances are toxic, many people persist in maintaining strong connections to people despite knowing they are toxic to their emotional or spiritual bodies. We cannot assume everyone wants to be well. We do not have the right to decide which relationships should be severed.

In addition to obtaining the client's permission before cutting cords, the psychic would do well to obtain or persuade the client to make a commitment to the process of letting go of unhealthy cords. If the client is not truly committed to letting go of ties that bind, the cords may reattach themselves after the healing, and the healer may find that they must work again and again to detach them. If, on some level, the client wants to remain attached to toxic people, removing the cords will only provide temporary relief. In such cases, the healer will have to decide if cutting the cords is a waste of time. Sometimes cutting the cords can provide the client with a taste of freedom, and this might convince them to consider committing to completely detaching themselves from the toxic relationships in their lives. On the other hand, if they have grown dependent on their connection to a particular toxic individual, suddenly removing that energy can cause a profound shock to their system. In the same way that suddenly stopping a drug can cause negative withdrawal symptoms, the sudden cutting of a cord can cause emotional withdrawal symptoms. For this reason, take care before and after cutting a cord.

QUESTION #9: CAN I JUST SEND EVERYONE TO THE LIGHT?

Some clients who come to a healer are contending with conditions externally imposed on them. There are some emotional and mental health conditions that are caused by or aggravated by the pressure of nonphysical entities. Earthbound spirits, astral beings, thoughtforms, spells, and demons can all be attached to a client's aura. The healer who has the gift of sight can see these entities, and if she does aura cleansing or spirit release work, she may want to remove these attachments and send them to the light. But all attachments do not necessarily get sent to the light.

After we die, our physical and etheric bodies decay and our astral body and other energy bodies live on. When we leave our physical body behind, we ascend to nonphysical realms beyond the physical one. Upon our departure from the physical, we will see a light guiding us to higher realms. A soul that follows the light will ascend to higher realms. Those souls that do not follow the light can get stuck on the Earth plane and become earthbound spirits, hungry ghosts, or beings who haunt the living. Mediums and healers are often able to see this guiding light and can direct lost souls to it. The light represents higher realms where higher-energy beings like angels reside. Often, the best way to help a lost soul or the best way to address negative energy is to "send it to the light" in the parlance of mediums.

Earthbound spirits, it can be argued, should be sent to the light as that is where they were always supposed to go. *Earthbound spirits* are the spirits of deceased people who, for various reasons, failed to leave the earth plane after they left their bodies. Usually, such spirits stick around because they are attached to or addicted to some aspect of physical life. Spirits may stay because 1) they died suddenly as the result of murder or an accident and refuse to accept that they are dead; 2) they died unexpectedly and think their death was unfair or want to see justice done in their case; 3) they died by suicide or caused their own death through carelessness or disregard for life and feel guilty about this so they stick around to punish themselves by watching the suffering their death has caused others; 4) they were addicted to alcohol, drugs, food, or sex and want to stick around so they can enjoy these addictions vicariously or directly through other people; 5) they are obsessed with their possessions—their homes, land, money, cars—and they stay on Earth to guard these items; or 6) they feel a desire or obligation to assist a friend or family member they have left behind.

Although it is almost always the case that earthbound spirits of type 4 (addicts) and 5 (materialists) need to be encouraged to go to the light, the other types may need to stick around for a while to complete a mission designed to assist in their soul growth, the soul growth of friends and family, or others. Eventually all earthbound spirits do need to be sent to the light, but sometimes the timing of their departure is key.

When it comes to thoughtforms, astral beings, spells, and demons, it may seem obvious that they should all be removed and sent to the light, but this is not always the case. First of all, as previously mentioned, it is important to get your client's consent before removing anything. Without consent, you may find that the entities return. If the client has an attachment to the entities and does not truly want them removed, they can also return after being removed. After obtaining permission, the second aspect of attachment the psychic-healers ought to concern themselves with is its purpose. When it comes to thoughtforms, for example, some people recite mantras, affirmations, or prayers that congeal into thoughtforms in their aura. These thoughtforms are helpful to the client and generally assist them in maintaining a certain positive perspective in life. One example is the violet flame mantra: "I am a being of cause alone. That cause is love, the sacred tone." Other examples include "I am a child of God," or "The universe is conspiring on my behalf." Repetition of these phrases can produce positive thoughtforms in the client's aura. Other thoughtforms, however, that are more frequently the result of unconscious repetition of thoughts, are harmful to the person and serve no beneficial purpose. These include thoughtforms like the following: "I'm fat," "Nobody loves me," "I always mess up," "Life is unfair," "Everything is a struggle." Because these thoughtforms are injurious and serve no purpose for the client, they should be removed.

The test of purpose is one that has to be performed before you remove any entities. If astral beings are attached to a person, the healer should ask them who they are and what their purpose is. If you ask an entity if it is there for the highest good of _____ (client's name), they will have to answer truthfully. If they are not there for the highest good of the client, they should be directed to the light. An example of a being that may not want or need to go to the light is a guardian angel or protector spirit. Some people have beings with them who are there to protect them. If these beings are indeed fulfilling the goal of providing protection, the client may want them to stay.

An exception to the rule that beings must answer questions posed to them about their purpose relates to demons. Demons are adept at deception and misrepresentation. It takes a highly trained psychic-healer to be able to negotiate with a demon. Healers who have not been properly prepared are warned against doing work of this kind. Not only will demons frequently lie about their identity and origin, they are also not keen on going to the light. Making an attempt to send a demon to the light or binding a demon can cause the psychic-medium to incur demonic retribution. This occurs when angry demons take revenge against healers by creating accidents, injuries, or even possession of the healer or her friends and family. Don't try to be Buffy the Demon Slayer without proper training and protection, and if you do not know how to distinguish demons from other maleficent spirits, do not attempt to remove entities.

QUESTION #10: DOES CALLING SPIRITS HURT THEM?

When I was young, I got involved in using a Ouija board while playing with three of my college mates. Because two of the four of us (one other girl and I) were natural [albeit untrained] mediums, we were able to bring through spirits clearly and consistently. For several weeks, we focused our attention on one particular spirit, R, who was able to provide information that we could verify. She made predictions that came true. We were having a lot of fun talking to her until she decided to try to take possession of the other medium (and my best friend). Although I was able to successfully remove the spirit from my friend, this incident scared us all enough to get us to stop playing this "game."

That semester a psychic was a guest on our college TV show that I helped produce. I took advantage of the opportunity to take her aside and ask her advice about calling spirits. She told me it was never a good idea to call spirits or to use a Ouija board, as there was no telling what kind of spirit might come. She also told me that Ouija board–type games were notorious for attracting the lowest type of earthbound spirit, and for that reason, they ought to be avoided. In my subsequent training at the hands of many spiritualist mediums, I heard it often repeated that one ought not to "call" spirits. The mediums that trained me taught me to tell clients that there was no guarantee that the particular spirit the client wanted to speak to would show up. We were only to speak to those spirits who, in effect, called on us. Of course, not all mediums believe you should avoid calling particular spirits, but many do. I have come to the conclusion after many years of experience working as a medium that only very experienced mediums with proper protections in place should request to speak to specific spirits.

Whether you are using a Ouija board or any other type of instrument, it is never a good idea to call out for unspecified spirits to come speak with you. Nor should you call out to spirits with whom you have no connection. If you have a client who wants to speak to one of their deceased relatives, you should be able to call on them, provided you are careful not to interrupt them in their Other World activities. If they are already earthbound, you must be careful not to encourage them to remain earthbound by making them feel so needed that they don't want to leave. Also, you must know how to distinguish the spirit of the deceased relative from other interlopers who might try to masquerade as the relative in order to gain an audience with you or your client.

When you're calling a spirit down to Earth, you need to be aware of whether or not you are interrupting their growth work on other planes. If your gift is not developed enough for you to discern such things you should not call them down by name. It is better to speak to those who come calling on their own. As a precaution, when calling spirits down to Earth, a psychic-medium can ask the spirit if speaking to the living aligns with their purpose and if it is interrupting their soul growth activities. Some spirits who are frequently called back to Earth to speak to loved ones may delay moving on and thus delay their own spiritual growth. The psychic/medium should be mindful of this possibility and should look for evidence that the visits are benefitting the deceased as well as the living.

QUESTION #11: WHEN IS IT OKAY TO PREDICT THE FUTURE?

Because of the attachment that humans have to three-dimensional reality, gifts that seem to defy the laws of physics are often the most impressive. Two supersensory gifts that are spectacular in this regard are precognition (prophecy) and telekinesis (moving objects with your mind). Precognition impresses and shocks people because it questions one of our fundamental beliefs: that time is linear and unidirectional. Similarly, telekinesis challenges our belief in the solidity of objects and their tendency to follow the laws of physics.

Because precognition is such a spectacular gift that has the potential to change a person's worldview, many psychics are encouraged to make predictions to prove their gift. Because predictions can easily be verified or found to be false by simply waiting for them to come to pass (or not), they provide an excellent form of feedback for prophet-psychics and their clients. When a psychic makes a successful prediction, she can turn a skeptic into a believer. If the psychic is making predictions in order to convince people that super senses are real, that may be a very good motive. Similarly, if a psychic is making predictions in order to warn a client of a preventable misfortune, that is also a good motive.

QUESTION # 12: IS IT OKAY TO READ PEOPLE ANYTIME, ANYWHERE?

If a person has the ability to deliver spontaneous psychic readings on demand anywhere, for anyone, should they? Is it okay to walk up to random people and read them?

A psychic, especially one who is new to the art, may find herself flooded with information about friends, family, coworkers, and even strangers. The psychic may feel compelled to share the information whenever she receives it. Such spontaneous sharing can be helpful and healing for the recipient, but it can also be harmful.

Some people will resent having their privacy violated by a psychic who knows things about them that they haven't shared or that they don't even know about themselves. Then, too, if you are reading someone in a public place (at work, at a bus stop, at the grocery store, at a family gathering), there is a chance you will share private information within earshot of others, thus possibly embarrassing your unofficial client. You also run the risk of your reading revealing secrets or identifying deceptions. In a spontaneous random reading, you may not have the time to tune in to the client to determine what they are ready to hear before delivering the message. Also, in a random reading with someone you do not know, or who you do not see often or have a close relationship with, you may not have the chance to do follow up work with them to ensure they are okay after the reading.

If, as I have recommended, your primary motivation for doing the work is to be of service, you must be careful about doing readings for strangers at times when they may not be prepared to receive or process the information. Are you providing the reading to be of service, or are you showing off or seeking to vent yourself of excess information? Are you just seeking to practice your craft? Is the reading more about you satisfying your needs than satisfying those of your client? These are questions that must be answered.

Dannion Brinkley, an author and near-death experiencer, developed psychic abilities after his first near-death experience, and for a while, he would use them in various ways—sometimes going up to strangers and reading them on the spot. He learned over time not to do this. He explains it in this way:

> Having psychic abilities means you have access to a person's most tender spots, the areas of his life that are most shielded from public view. "Seeing" the areas is sometimes good because it gives people a chance to talk freely about the pain in their lives. The problem is that people don't always want to talk about the pain in their lives, least of all with a stranger who tells them things a stranger shouldn't know.[3]

Another possible problem with doing random readings concerns the value or lack of value that you or your unofficial clients may place on your gift. In our society, gifts and services that are given away are often valued less than those that are sold. The value ascribed to your gift matters if you want to maximize your effectiveness in the world. People who value a service are more likely to take it seriously and to follow the guidance you offer, whereas many people dismiss the importance of information or a service they have received for free. In the same way that people are prone to disregard unsolicited advice, if the person has not asked you to read them, they may not be particularly interested in your unsolicited reading. Not only will the undervalued or unvalued reading potentially fail to provide any real service to the client, but it may also prove a disservice to you, the psychic.

If psychics are tiring themselves out by offering free spontaneous readings everywhere, all the time, they may find it hard to value what they do. Not valuing what they do could have numerous negative impacts for them. They may fail to take their gift seriously enough to develop it and hone it. They may not have enough energy to do their paid readings if they are overtired from being "on" all day, every day. Because such psychics are delivering readings to people who have not asked for them, might not believe in them, and may not value them, they may find that these "clients" also may not follow their advice and, as a result, they may not receive feedback regarding the helpfulness and accuracy of the reading that they need in order to grow.

Doing charity work is important and I strongly recommend psychics offer free and discount services to persons who need them. But offerings should be conducted with the same ceremony and seriousness as paid readings. Clients should set appointments and prepare themselves for said appointments. The psychic should set aside time and space to conduct the reading and prepare to deliver it. Designating a special time and place, and choosing certain tools, decorations, music, art, and clothing allows the psychic to signal to Spirit, the clients, and to themself that they take the work seriously; the more seriously the psychic takes their work, the stronger their work will become.

Famed psychic-medium John Holland talks about how, when he first got started, he used to go up to random strangers and read them. He learned over time that this was not right. He writes, "Nowadays, I advise people who believe they have special abilities to *never* walk up to a stranger and start giving them information like this. To put it bluntly, I was untrained and inexperienced, and I'm sure I came across as downright rude at times. There's an ethical responsibility when you do this work."[4]

QUESTION # 13: CAN'T I JUST LISTEN TO SPIRIT (AND NOT CLIENTS OR COLLEAGUES)?

Psychic-healers who are psychic-mediums may rely on guidance from Spirit or spirits to do their work. Those with strong Spirit guidance may have learned over time that the more they adhere to the guidance they receive from Spirit, the more successful and helpful their work will be. Developing one's gift as a medium involves learning how to listen intently and with focus in order to faithfully interpret the guidance or message from Spirit. A medium who has an excellent connection to reliable Spirit or God guidance may be tempted to disregard the guidance or feedback they receive from humans, especially if it does not match the information they obtain from Spirit. This can be a problem for the following reasons:

1. When a medium values Spirit communication above all other communications, they are assuming they are 100 percent accurate in how they receive and interpret the messages. As stated earlier, the very best psychics in the world tend to be about 80 to 90 percent accurate, so a 100 percent accuracy rate is extremely unlikely. This means that even if Spirit is never wrong, the psychic occasionally is. Thus, 20 percent of the time, unless they are open to feedback, when the psychic is wrong about the guidance they think they are getting, they do not know they are wrong.

2. Anyone in a human body has chosen to incarnate on the Earth plane in order to experience Earth life. Earth life experience includes communicating with and relating to other earthlings. If a soul comes to Earth but focuses all of their attention on Spirit and fails to engage fully with other human beings, the question might arise as to why they came to Earth at all.

3. If your motivation, as a psychic, is to be of service, it is going to be important for you to listen to your clients to ensure that you are actually serving them. If the clients disagree with what you claim Spirit advises, then you will have to address that discrepancy in order to truly help them.

4. Your colleagues, and some of your clients, have their own Spirit guidance. You have no reason to assume that your spirits or your mystic connection is more reliable than that of your colleagues'. You cannot assume that you have a more evolved or enlightened soul than your colleagues and all of your clients.

The ethical psychic remains humble and open to learning. Listening to advice and guidance from your colleagues allows you to get feedback on your work and to learn from your mistakes. To say that you do not need feedback from your colleagues betrays an arrogance that can cripple your growth and the development of your gifts. To say that Spirit is always right is another way of saying "I am always right" because you are assuming that you always interpret what Spirit is telling you correctly.

QUESTION #14: DO I NEED TO BE TRAINED TO BE A PSYCHIC?

Some psychics are born with all of their gifts and express them from childhood. Others manifest them slowly over time. Being born with gifts doesn't mean you should avoid training any more than being born with a great singing voice means you should avoid voice training. Excellence comes with practice and honing of your gift so although you may not *need* training to be a psychic, you need it to become an ethical psychic. All psychics, regardless of their gift, can gain more control over their gift with training of some kind. Specializations also require training. You may have natural gifts of clairvoyance , mediumship, clairaudience, and so on, but you may have not yet learned how to use those gifts as a psychic detective solving crimes or as a medical intuitive identifying illness.

The ethical psychic avoids claiming that they have specialized gifts or that they practice modalities that they have not been trained in. Clients are not just drawn to certain modalities because they are popular. They are drawn to them because they are a match to the vibration of the name of the modality or because they have received guidance to pursue a certain type of healing. If you claim to be doing something you are not, you are obstructing that client from receiving the type of assistance that they require. If you want to be a medium, train to be one. If you want to be a medical intuitive, study under an established medical intuitive.

As famed psychic-medium John Edward explains, "You can't *act* like you are a psychic . . . you have to be it for real, sincere and straight from the heart. You can be no one else but you and can use only the abilities you have at your disposal. If you are not born a medium, you are not a medium. If you are just starting out developing your intuition, you are not ready to give readings."[5]

QUESTION # 15: WHAT DO I DO IF
I THINK MY CLIENT IS MENTALLY ILL?

Sometimes people with mental health issues are attracted to psychics even though they actually need therapy. Sometimes these clients have had a bad experience with a psychotherapist, have a negative attitude about therapy, or are afraid of the stigma of receiving therapy. Sometimes mentally ill clients can be helped by visiting a healer, but only if the psychic-healer is attuned to the client's special needs. It is important that the psychic be aware of their limitations in addressing mental illness in a client.

Mentally ill clients can pose a danger to themselves and others when their conditions are not properly treated. If, as a psychic-healer, you are not also trained in mental health, you should not attempt to provide informal therapy to your client. Be prepared to refer them to a therapist and do not attempt to rationalize with them when they become irrational. Someone without a mental illness can be talked into being reasonable, but when someone has a chemical imbalance, their behavior will not necessarily be predictable, and they will not necessarily respond to direction.

There is much more at stake with a mentally ill person. If you say the wrong thing, you can trigger a meltdown, a psychotic break, a manic episode, a depressive episode, violence, or suicide. For this reason, a psychic who recognizes that a client may have a mental illness should proceed with extreme caution and should not attempt to play the role of therapist. If your suggestion to the client is that they seek professional mental health assistance but they disregard your advice, you may need to cease contact with the client until they follow through on said treatment. Knowing your limitations as a psychic and working within those limits will ensure that you are able to help the most people and hurt the fewest.

QUESTION #16: CAN I DIAGNOSE AN ILLNESS?

There are many countries where psychic diagnosis is accepted, but the laws in the United States prevent anyone who is not licensed as a medical professional from diagnosing illness or prescribing medicine. Find out what the laws are in your country. "But what if I am a medical intuitive?" you might ask. Aren't people counting on you to diagnose their problem and offer a treatment solution? Medical intuitives have become popular in recent years precisely because people have not gotten the answers they seek from licensed medical practitioners. A medical intuitive may indeed receive information that identifies, confirms, or disconfirms a diagnosis or treatment plan. In such cases, the psychic must explain clearly to the client that she is not a licensed medical practitioner and that the information being provided is for educational purposes only. The client should be encouraged to seek out a licensed medical professional, and you should make sure they understand that your services do not serve as a substitute for medical assistance. If you present medical intuition as an adjunct therapy, as information that the client can combine with information they are receiving from their healthcare providers, then you avoid violating the law or endangering the client's health.

That being said, the reason that medical intuition is such a popular modality is precisely because it offers something that is currently lacking in mainstream healthcare. Clients coming to medical intuitives often come because they have not received a diagnosis from their healthcare provider, they have received a diagnosis that doesn't offer them hope, or they have been given a treatment for their condition that does not work. Even some clients who are happy with the medical care they have gotten still feel they need more information than their doctor can offer them. Medical intuition can address these issues; it can explain why certain diagnoses have not helped the client, and it can explain why a particular treatment is not working for a particular person. It can also address emotional and spiritual aspects of illness that are not included in conventional healthcare. So, although in some countries, a medical intuitive is prohibited by law from giving a diagnosis, and it is important not to discourage a client from getting proper medical care, it is possible to help them in many ways that add to what they are already receiving from other healthcare providers without officially "diagnosing" them.

QUESTION # 17: HOW DO I SET
FAIR PRICES FOR MY SERVICES?

Many people in the helping professions are challenged by the question of what to charge their clients. Because of widespread beliefs about the mixing of money and service, figuring out what to charge can create special problems for the psychic-healer. Although people generally believe that nobody should work for free and that work done well deserves payment, we have a counterintuitive tendency in the West to expect to pay more for non-helping services than for helping ones. Thus teachers, counselors, and social workers are paid much lower wages than entertainers, technicians, and even laborers. There is a societal consensus that people in certain helping fields should not expect to be paid or should not expect to be paid well for helping others. Many people expect that those who pick such fields do so because they are giving from their heart and are not hoping to become rich. We even expect certain fields to not charge for services at all. In fact, some people believe that a true healer should never charge for her services. The same expectation, strangely, does not apply to doctors who charge exorbitant prices for their services, regardless of whether or not they help their patient. Healers are often expected to donate their services despite the fact that they also need to house and clothe and feed themselves to live.

In some Indigenous cultures, medicine people traditionally did not charge a fee. However, in those cultures, the medicine person was completely supported by the tribe or village: their food, shelter, and clothing were provided so they could focus on healing. In the United States, some tribes are returning to these old ways and supporting their medicine people with salaries or food and housing so they do not need to charge their clients.

Western society's general undervaluing of service work, combined with our tendency to expect healers to work for free, is compounded by a long history of people (particularly in religious contexts) using their gifts to manipulate and exploit others. Preachers, ministers, self-proclaimed gurus and yogis, pretend medicine men, and magician-mediums have used their gifts and promoted fear to get money and sexual favors from their clients and congregations. Such persons have stained the reputations of all psychic-healers, resulting in widespread suspicion of anyone claiming to offer their supersensory gifts in exchange for money.

The psychic who is trying to set a fair price is often influenced by these attitudes, beliefs, histories, and suspicions and, as a result, she may find it difficult to charge the fee her services truly merit. It is important for the psychic to resist allowing these beliefs and prejudices to prevent her from making a living. If a psychic has internalized any of the following beliefs, she will need to do the emotional work to rid herself of these limiting ideas:

1. I shouldn't charge for using my gifts.

2. Healers should work for free or charge very little.

3. It is wrong to get rich helping people.

4. If my fees are high, I am charging too much and exploiting my clients.

In addition to addressing these internalized societal beliefs about healer fees, many psychic-healers will want to address and process past-life vows of poverty that are influencing their present life. Once these emotional and spiritual concerns are addressed, the psychic should price her work according to the standards that apply to all types of work. The price should be determined by:

1. The quality of the service provided.

2. The experience and training of the provider.

3. How the provider ranks compared to the competition.

If you are better-trained and more experienced—that is, if you are a psychic-healer who has taken classes or undergone training (formally or informally) to develop and hone your gift—you should charge more.

It is just as important to avoid overcharging for your services. If you are an untrained psychic or are just starting out, you should charge less than what you will be able to charge after you get trained or gain several years' experience. Regardless of how gifted you may believe yourself to be, you should recognize that when you first begin doing readings or healings, you are still at the learning stage of your career. You are, in effect, an intern or an apprentice who is honing your craft through practice. As such, you should not expect to charge high rates for effectively learning from your clients. Recognize that, at this stage, you are being paid less than a professional because you are still developing. As you progress in your field, your ability to deliver consistently reliable and helpful readings will improve. As you get more and more practice and get progressively better at what you do, raise your fees.

A beginning psychic, undergoing the practicum phase of their training, should be willing to work for less in order to gain experience in certain venues or to build their client list. At a certain stage, doing a large volume of free and low-paying readings is more valuable than doing a small number of high-paying readings because the junior psychic benefits from all the practice that multiple readings provide.

Once the apprenticeship period is over, the psychic should price their readings in accordance with their training, experience, and the feedback they have received. This cannot be stated enough: *a psychic should always take the feedback of clients and colleagues seriously*. If she has listened to the feedback she received in the early years of her career and learned from it, she should find her reviews greatly improve over time. If clients consistently say that her readings have transformed their lives, the psychic can feel comfortable pricing her services accordingly. If, on the other hand, her clients usually describe the psychic's readings as "interesting" or "fun," the psychic should price the readings according to what she thinks "fun" is worth.

Although a psychic may be tempted to give away her services or underprice them in what she sees as an act of charity, the ethical psychic must keep in mind that in the West people value most what they pay the most for and they often suspect inexpensive items of being inadequate in some way. When a person makes a financial investment in goods or services, they treat them better, they keep them longer, and they take better care of them. If a client spends a certain amount of money on a reading, they are more likely to follow through on the advice given in the reading because of their investment. In this way, the price of the reading actually contributes to the services provided and to the client's transformation. It is more difficult for the client to disregard what they have been told by the psychic after they have spent a non-negligible sum of money on the reading. Paying for a reading allows the client to express gratitude and demonstrate that they take it seriously. This is one of the reasons that Diné (Navajo) healing ceremonies are not cheap.[6]

The important thing where pricing is concerned is that the psychic clearly describes, in advance, the services they will provide to the client for the price they are charging. An ethical psychic does not lure a client in with one price and then add fees or talk a client into a higher-priced service after they have arrived. Upselling is not appropriate in psychic work where people are often coming to the psychic in desperation or distress. It is important that the psychic not take advantage of the client's misfortune. People who are desperate will often spend more than they can afford. It is the psychic's responsibility not to encourage this behavior. Along these same lines, it is not appropriate for a psychic to identify a problem that can only be fixed by paying for more services from the same psychic. Vulnerable clients should be nurtured, not exploited for further financial gain.

With regard to offering services, it is also important not to overpromise. Never claim to be 100 percent accurate, and never claim you are certain you can fix the clients problem, get them a job, heal their ailment, and so on. Guarantees cannot be made in intuitive work because intuitive work deals with energy and the psychic does not have control over the energy. The psychic also does not have control over the client's life. The psychic cannot always know in advance if it is even permissible for the client to be healed or if it is in alignment with their soul's purpose for their problem to be solved.

A final issue to consider in pricing readings concerns access. The price of a service will determine who has access to the service. You can effectively price out certain segments of the population and you may want to avoid that. How do you provide service to a wide cross-section of the population and still charge what your sessions are truly worth? The solution to this problem is to distinguish between business and charity. It is possible to do both, but it is not necessary to sacrifice one for the other. A psychic can charge high prices if that is what her client feedback warrants and can offer discounted or free sessions to the financially needy in a tithing mechanism wherein she provides free or discounted sessions to every tenth client. Alternatively, a psychic can provide free or discount readings at community or charity events or at community centers in low-income areas while still earning the bulk of her income from higher-priced readings targeted at wealthier clientele.

ACKNOWLEDGMENTS

This work would not have been possible without the assistance, counsel, and generosity of so many people, both living and dead.

Much gratitude to my students who inspired this book. Without their questions I never would have been inspired to write this book: Jim Sharp, Jeanette Staine, Farzana Nayani, Emi Hoshino, Mason Smith, Elizabeth Hallat, Michelle Schrocter, Sarah Holder, Amelia Vigil, and so many others in Los Angeles, Riverside, Altadena, Oakland, and remotely all over the world.

This writing could not have happened without artist grants from Zhayra Palma, Lekha Kanchinadam, Atava Garcia Swiecicki, the 6 Month Mutual Aid Society, and the Center for Cultural Innovation.

Thank you to my family: Robert E. Vest III, Julia Vest, JilChristina Vest, Timothy Walton, Carol Burnett Vest, Michele Lee Davis, Donna Rodriguez, Bianca Quiñones, and Bailey Quiñones for their generosity, support, and encouragement while I was writing.

I am ever grateful to my father for introducing me to so many wise teachers, for surrounding me with his psychic friends, and for connecting me to past-life regression and taking me to see the medical intuitive who urged me onto this path.

My mother's guidance on reading cards, on questioning authority, and on how to be a psychic without killing myself have been invaluable.

This book was revised in the wake of an accident and injury. During my recovery more people helped me than I can possibly recall by name. So many students, colleagues, friends, and family came out of the woodwork to assist me in a myriad of ways. I am especially indebted to my Women of Color Medicine Apprentices who secured a safe space for me to write and heal, ensuring I would be able to continue this work: to Porsche Combash, for finding housing for me, driving me north, looking after my beloved doggie, feeding me, and being my rock; to Lorena Pena, for her many gifts; to Gigi Valdes for her love, her financial support, and healing trips to the beach; to Fariha Naveed, for technical assistance; and to Rosi Bustamante and Artlyn Johnson for the herbal medicines.

Thank you to Julia Vest for editing the first draft of this manuscript, for all the soul-saving letters, your immediate and ongoing emotional and financial support during my recovery, and thank you for being a friend as much as a sister.

Thank you to spirit sister Elizabeth Philipose who helped in more ways than I can recount; Thank you to my brilliant and bold sister JilChristina for, among other things hauling furniture and building bookshelves so I would have a study in which to write; thank you to Ramona Laughing Brook, my Afro-Indigenous sister for healing journeys and for being a safe harbor in the storm.

Thank you to Miko Dieudonne for her constant support, to Farzana Nayani for connecting me to North Atlantic Books, to my artist brother Amrit Kohli who was there for me when it mattered most, and to Donald Gerard, my fellow spiritual scientist for supporting and believing in my dream. Thank you to Tracy Evangelista for food, crystals, and loyalty.

Special thanks to Marie Dutton Brown, my agent, for her sage advice, to Shayna Keyles, my editor, for putting up with me, to production editor, Trisha Peck, and the whole NAB publishing team for believing in this project; and much love for my coach Kristi Pallino, for helping me to stay focused on the grand plan.

Portions of this book were written at the Questhaven Retreat Center in San Marcos, California. I am grateful to the kindhearted and welcoming staff there: Blake Isaac, Laurie Jablon-Burke, Randy Nixon, Larry Frizzell, Becky Thompson, and especially my teacher, Gordon Bleth. Thank you for all the impromptu lessons on the path, Gordon!

I want to say *Shonobash* to the following people for bringing me food, healing, prayers, for giving me rides to the doctors and the vets, acupuncture, and physical rehab, for helping me to move, for GoFundMe donations, and for your love and support during my long recovery after the car accident. Because of your help I was able to heal and finish this book: Erika Rincon, Tracy Evangelista, Maria Kovanko, Emi Hoshino, Claudia Rueda, Dr. Elizabeth Philipose, Julia Vest, Jim Sharp, Kaycee Wysaski, Nikole Fiamengo, Betsy Vega, Carol Killian, Johana Moran, Lisa Strack, Margaret So, Ingrid De Santiago, Kelly Albano, Masha Kovanko, Michelle Schroeter, Matthew Mason, Kimberlynn Acevedo, Constance Slider Pierre, Patrick Vogel, Gregory Curry, Tiffany Tonel, Mary Vu, Taikera Conyers, J Pham, Monique Jimenez, Lisa Chang, Darcey Iwashita, Phoenix Two Spirit Bennett, Lynn Jimenez, Olivia Shakir, Princess, Denise Pinon, Pj, Destiny Grant, Marlon Fixico, Winnifred Paul, Joely Gomez, Kiana Rose, Sara Bailey, Sosa, Karen Rodriguez, Corinne Smith, Dan Stradford, Christa Bell, Justin Elledge, Farzana Nayani, Susan Eriksen, Fiona Carlone, Flossie Park, Maya Sakya, Roger Kuhn, Victoria Bomberry, Sarah Holder, Amelia Vigil, Mike Combash, Rene Roman, Izzy Asencion, Laila Bahman, Seemi Ghazi, JN, Shabnam Piryaei, Mason Smith, Jess H, Cindi Mayweather, Rebecca Duffy, Michelle Olaya-Marquez, Mitsuyo Hosoyama, Kaycee Krieg, Tanya Ramirez, Lidia Sebhat, Artlyn Johnson, Carrie Schell, Sarah Wolfarth-Davis, Grisel Torres, Akudo Mez, Dr. Jasmine Bauknight, Cassandra Daisy, Anne Trakas, Deborah Garcia Negrete, Enitan Marcelle, Laurina Laupase, Judy J, Adriana Adorno, Alisa Lofton, Muriel Vinson, Giacoma Pluma, Irene Kaludi, Romel Salcedo, Lyn Alicia Henderson, Danica Schutz, Kira Haling, Lisa Medina, Mary Newson, Emily Ruff, Josie Santiago,

Gina Wesley, Brandi Miss, Jane Paik, Daphne Garcia, Latoya Clark, Faith Nouri, Edyka Chilome, Zochitl Bernadette, Manav Thaper, Jill Curtis, Lisa Chen, Elizabeth Hallet, Pagan George, Hilja Keading, Blair Bogin, Garrett Stevens, Gasselle Rodriguez, Daria Garina, Karo Sana, Kathryn Sorrells, Raquel Gutierrez, Santee Wilson, Marcel Nagy, Omunique Amey, Fariha Naveed, Noosha Kahali, Erika Martinez, Fanesia Vienna, Melissa Monte, Sita Fischer, Umma Amina, Deborah Gregory, Laurie Allesandra, Shanique Abrams, Gabrielle Muzac, Kesi McCarthy-Brown, Rebeca Parker, Jasmine Ureno-Diaz, Angela Gallegos, Ayanna Maia, Jennifer Farmer, Caroline Valverde, Natalia Vigil, Donna Rodriguez, Natalie Gomez, Emerald Tlatoani, Robin Powell, Dorina Michelle, Cynthi Lynes, Judith, Dandilion Cloverdale, Anitheiess Jackson, Noni Session, Danielle Gailey, Empress Shenai Chung, Marie Anderson, Tahirah Carter, Joseph, Becca the dogwalker, Dhannel Azada Rocker, Dr. Tina Fernades Botts, Dr. Caldwell, Yeshe Mathews, Allison Rosen Vogel, Diane Ross, Ahimsa Timoteo Bodhrán, Farah Zeb, Siri Gillespie, Gretchen Grathwohl, Dawn Haney, Berkeley Food Pantry, Soltree Alchemy, Optimal Performance and Recovery, Flint Rehab, Wowlvenn Seward-Katzmiller, Joshua Darnell, Lulu Love, Samantha Thornhill, and Cathy Deppe.

Finally, I would like to thank my many teachers, both human and spirit, who have taught me so much: LulaMae Collins Vest, Michele Lee Davis Vest, Robert E. Vest Jr., Dr. Leonard Vest, Dr. James Vest, Saundra Hall Vest, Mother Joyce Cuff, Mother Mavis White, Mother Mary "Cuz" Brown, Sister and Elder Barrett, Mother Viola Williams, Sister Carole Robinson, Sister Sampleton, Mother White, Sister Nelson, Sister Alice King, M. P. Taylor, Mrs. Taylor, Nyah, Inez, Anthony, Devon, Mother Taylor, Maeda Jones, Mary Rose Gray, Kathy Groseclose, Suzanne DeWeez, Stephen Atkins, Don Little Cloud Davenport, Bonita Sizemore, Zenobia Embry, Tall Oak Weeden, Dr. Erna Brodber, Phoenix Bennett,

Dr. Barbara Christian, Joan Piper, Michelle Hayes, Reverend William Killian, Reverend Q. Gerald Roseberry, the Ghazi family of Skokie, Illinois, Elijah Powell, my Spirit Guides Ebim, Standing Warrior, and Silas, archangels Rafael, Metatron, Gabriel, and Raziel, and my council.

NOTES

INTRODUCTION

1 Ann Ree Colton, *Ethical ESP* (Marina Del Rey, CA: DeVorss, 1971), 18.

2 Manly P. Hall, *Magic: A Treatise on Esoteric Ethics* (Los Angeles: The Philosophical Research Society, 1978, 1998), 15.

CHAPTER 1

1 Thomas E. Mails (in dialogue with Sioux Holy Man Fools Crow), *Fools Crow: Wisdom and Power* (Tulsa: Council Oak Books, 1991), 40.

2 Joyce Elaine Noll, *Company of Prophets: African American Psychics, Healers, and Visionaries,* 2nd ed. (New York: Llewellyn, January 1, 1992), 51.

3 John Edward, *Infinite Quest: Develop Your Psychic Intuition to Take Charge of Your Life* (New York: Sterling, 2010), 252.

4 Allison DuBois, *We Are Their Heaven: Why the Dead Never Leave Us* (Palmer, AK: Fireside, 2006), 121.

5 According to the Spiritualists' National Union, a body that oversees all the spiritualist churches in the United Kingdom, "The main aim of mediumship is to provide evidence of survival of the human personality beyond physical death." Accessed March 8, 2022, https://www.snu.org.uk/about-us.

6 "Core Shamanism," The Foundation for Shamanic Studies, accessed January 13, 2022, https://shamanism.org/workshops/coreshamanism.html.

7 "We've researched and ranked the best shamanism books in the world, based on recommendations from world experts, sales data, and

millions of reader ratings." Shortform, "100 Best Shamanism Books of All Time," accessed March 8, 2022, https://www.shortform.com /best-books/genre/best-shamanism-books-of-all-time.

8   For more on neoshamnism, white shamans, and Harnerism, see Geary Hobson, "The Rise of the White Shaman as a New Version of Cultural Imperialism," In Gary Hobson (ed.), *The Remembered Earth* (Red Earth Press: Albuquerque, NM, 1978). 100–10.; Geary Hobson, "The Rise of the White Shaman: Twenty-Five Years Later," *Studies in American Indian Literatures* Series 2, Vol. 14, No. 2/3 (Summer/Fall 2002): 1–11; and Joseba I. Arregi, "Plastic Shamans, Intellectual Colonialism and Intellectual Appropriation in New Age Movements," *The International Journal of Ecopsychology (IJE)*Volume 2, Issue 1, Article 10, April 30, 2021, https://digitalcommons.humboldt.edu/ije/vol2/iss1/10.

9   See, for example, the roster of sound healers that teach at sound healing schools and present at conferences: Globe Healing Institute, accessed January 13, 2022, https://globalhealinginstitute.org.

10 Chloé Meley, "The TikTokers Calling Out Spiritual Appropria-tion," *Huck* (online), April 29, 2021, https://www.huckmag.com /perspectives/activism-2/the-tiktokers-calling-out-spiritual -appropriation/.

11 Jess Joho and Morgan Sung, "How to Be a Witch without Stealing Other People's Cultures: Witchcraft Is More Than a Trendy TikTok Aesthetic," Mashable, October 31, 2020, https://mashable.com /article/witchtok-problematic-witch-cultural-appropriation.

12 Dr. Erika Buenaflor, *Cleansing Rites of Curanderismo: Limpias Espir-ituales of Ancient Mesoamerican Shamans* (Rochester, VT: Bear and Company, 2018), 91.

13 Freya Rey, *The Ethical Psychic: A Survival Guide for the Professional Psychic* (CreateSpace Independent Publishing Platform, June 20, 2011).

14 Thomas G. West, *Plato's "Apology of Socrates": An Interpretation, with a New Translation* (Ithaca, NY: Cornell University Press, 1979).

15 Susan Schuster Campbell, *Called to Heal: African Shamanic Healers* (Twin Lakes, WI: Lotus Press, 1998), 80.

16 Campbell, *Called to Heal*, 24.

17 A bad jinn is "a class of being that is neither angel nor spirit of the dead." Konstatinos, *Summoning Spirits: The Art of Magical Evocation* (St. Paul, MN: Llewellyn Publications, September 8, 2002). For more about jinns, see Baal Kadmon, *How to Bind the Jinn to Do Your Bid-ding* (Createspace Publishing, 2015). In Islamic Cosmology, there are

also "good" jinn. See Vivian A. Laughlin, "A Brief Overview of *al Jinn* within Islamic Cosmology and Religiosity," *Journal of Adventist Mission Studies* 11, No. 1, Art. 9 (2015).

18 For a more comprehensive introduction to magickal arts, see Donald Michael Kraig, *Modern Magick: Eleven Lessons in the High Magickal Arts* (St. Paul, MN: Llewellyn Publications, 1988).)

19 Peter Brown, as quoted by Joyce Elaine Noll in *Company of Prophets: African American Psychics, Healers, and Visionaries* (St. Paul, MN: Llewellyn Publications, 1991), 38.

CHAPTER 2

1 Janet Nohavec, *Where Two Worlds Meet: How to Develop Evidential Mediumship* (San Diego: Aventine Press, 2010), 27.

2 Alexandra Chauran, *The Ethics and Responsibilities of Being a Psychic* (New York: Llewelyn Worldwide, 2013). Kindle Edition, Location 29.

3 Chauran, *Ethics and Responsibilities.*

4 Penelope Quest, *Reiki for Life: The Complete Guide to Reiki Practice for Levels 1, 2, and 3* (New York: Tarcher/Perigee, 2016), 279.

5 Colette Baron-Reid, "Top 3 Elements of a Reputable Psychic!" [Blog], October 17, 2012, https://www.colettebaronreid.com/2012/10/17/top-3-elements-of-a-reputable-psychic/.

6 Santeria Church of the Orishas "SAFE," accessed March 10, 2021, http://santeriachurch.org/santeros-against-fraud-and-exploitation/.

7 Santeria Church of the Orishas "SAFE: Code of Ethics/Conduct," accessed March 10, 2021, http://santeriachurch.org/santeros-against-fraud-and-exploitation/.

8 Mercy Manci, Xhosa healer and founder of Nyangayezizwe Traditional Doctors Organization, as quoted in Susan Schuster Campbell, *Called To Heal: African Shamanic Healers* (Twin Lakes, WI: Lotus Press, 1998), 111.

9 For more on what occurs in a pre-life conference see Robert Schwartz, *Your Souls Plan: Discovering the Real Meaning of the Life You Planned Before You Were Born* (Berkeley, CA: North Atlantic Books, 2009).

10 Allison DuBois is the medium whose real-life experiences working with police to solve crimes inspired the hit TV show, *The Medium.*

CHAPTER 3

1 John Edward, *Infinite Quest: Develop Your Psychic Intuition to Take Charge of Your Life* (New York: Sterling, 2010), 38–39.

2 Raymond Buckland, *Buckland's Complete Book of Witchcraft* (Woodbury, MN: Llewelyn, 2011), 13.

3 Megan Lane, "Hoodoo Heritage: A Brief History of American Folk Religion" (master's thesis, University of Georgia, 2008); 49–50.

4 Lane, "Hoodoo Heritage." She cites Lawrence W. Levine, *Black Culture and Black Consciousness* (New York: Oxford University Press, 2007), 71–72 and Jeffrey E. Anderson, *Conjure in African American Society* (Baton Rouge, LA: Louisiana State University Press, 2005), 63.

5 Willow, "Spellcrafting Series: To Curse or Not to Curse; Ethics in Spellcrafting," *Flying the Hedge: The Path of a Hedgewitch* [Blog], June 23, 2021, https://www.flyingthehedge.com/2021/06/ethics-in-witchcraft.html.

6 Erika Buenaflor, *Cleansing Rites of Curanderismo: Limpias Espirituales Ancient Mesoamerican Shamans* (Rochester VT: Bear and Company, 2018), 100.

7 Doris Agee, *Edgar Cayce on ESP* (New York: Paperback Library, 1969), 78–79.

8 A glamour spell allows a witch to create an illusion so that others see her in whatever way she wants them to.

9 Manly P. Hall. *Magic: A Treatise on Esoteric Ethics* (Los Angeles: Philosophical Research Society, January 1, 1998), 23.

10 Hall, *Magic*, 44.

11 Maya Warrier, "Guru Choice and Spiritual Seeking in Contemporary India," *International Journal of Hindu Studies* 7 (February 2003): 31–54, https://doi.org/10.1007/s11407-003-0002-7.

12 Jayaram V, "The Tradition of Sat Guru in Hinduism," Hinduwebsite.com, accessed January 1, 2021, https://www.hinduwebsite.com/hinduism/concepts/guru.asp.

13 See, for example, Robert F. Berkhoffer, *The White Man's Indian: Images of the American Indian from Columbus to the Present* (New York: Vintage, 1979) and Terry Macy, Daniel Hart, Sonia Whittier, and Luana Ross, *White Shamans, Plastic Medicine Men: A Documentary*, produced by Terry Macy, Daniel Hart, Sonia Whittier, and Luana Ross (Bozeman, MT: Native Voices Public Television, 1996), DVD.

14 Bradford Keeney, "Walking Thunder: Dine Medicine Woman," in
    Nancy Connor, ed., with Bradford Keeney *Shamans of the World:*
    Extraordinary First-Person Accounts of Healings, Mysteries, and Miracles
    (Boulder, CO: Sounds True, 2008), 59.

15 Eliza Griswold, *Yoga Reconsiders the Role of the Guru in the Age of*
    #MeToo, New Yorker, July 23, 2019, https://www.newyorker.com/news
    /news-desk/yoga-reconsiders-the-role-of-the-guru-in-the-age-of-metoo.

16 Adrian Horton, "'He Got Away with It': How the Founder of Bikram
    Yoga Built an Empire on Abuse," *Guardian,* November 20, 2019,
    https://www.theguardian.com/film/2019/nov/20/bikram-choudhury
    -yoga-founder-abuse-netflix-documentary; Sabrina Barr, "Bikram
    Choudhury: Who Is the Yoga Guru Accused of Rape and Sexual Abuse?"
    Independent, November 20, 2019, https://www.independent.co.uk
    /life-style/bikram-choudhury-yoga-rape-sexual-abuse-netflix
    -documentary-who-a9210771.html.

17 Marc Lacy, "New Age Guru Guilty in Sweat Lodge Deaths," *New York*
    Times, June 22, 2011, https://www.nytimes.com/2011/06/23/us
    /23sweat.html.

18 Jayaram V, "The Tradition of Sat Guru."

19 "Shri Mataje Nirmala Devi: Q&A," TV Interview ORF, Vienna, Austria,
    December 10, 2019, https://www.sahajayoga.net.au/question-how
    -do-you-discriminate-a-false-guru-and-a-genuine-guru/. In recent
    years in India, there has been a crackdown on fake gurus who use
    their position to abuse their followers. Two prominent Hindu gurus
    have recently been convicted of rape. For example, see Bill Chappell,
    "Influential Guru Asaram Bapu Given Life Sentence for Raping Teen-
    age Girl," WBUR: NPR News, April 25, 2018, https://www.wbur.org
    /npr/605617921/indian-court-hits-influential-guru-asaram-bapu
    -with-life-sentence-for-rape-of-te

20 Lord Acton (John Emerich Edward Dalberg), Letter to Archbishop
    Mandell Creighton, Online Library of Liberty, April 5, 1887, https://
    history.hanover.edu/courses/excerpts/165acton.html.

CHAPTER 4

1 Charles W. Leadbeater, *The Astral Plane: Its Scenery, Inhabitants and*
   Phenomena (Project Gutenberg edition), 21; originally published in
   1895 by the Theosophical Society.

CHAPTER 5

1 Thomas E. Mails, *Fools Crow: Wisdom and Power* (Tulsa: Council Oak Books, 1991), 30.

2 For information on the long path monks must take before learning to manifest *siddhis*, or supernatural powers, see Arahant Upatissa, *The Path of Freedom—Vimuttimagga* (Colombo, Sri Lanka: The Saman Press, 1961). Or see Patañjali, *The Yoga Sutras of Patanjali: The Book of the Spiritual Man: An Interpretation* (London: Watkins, 1975).

3 Sonia Choquette, *Diary of a Psychic: Shattering the Myths* (Carlsbad, CA: Hay House, 2003); John Holland, *Born Knowing*, 2nd ed. (Carlsbad, CA: Hay House, 2003).

4 Alexandra Chauran, *The Ethics and Responsibilities of Being a Psychic* (Woodbury, MN: Llewellyn, 2013), 28.

5 "An Interview with Danny Billy," in Dagmar Thorpe, ed., *People of the Seventh Fire: Returning Lifeways of Native America* (Ithaca, NY: Akwe:kon/Cornell University American Indian Program, 1996), 22.

6 "Code of Ethics," Association of Independent Readers and Rootworkers (AIRR), accessed January 26, 2022, http://readersandrootworkers.org /wiki/Code_of_Ethics.

7 See the following studies: Florian Kurth, Nicolas Cherbuin, and Eileen Luders, "Promising Links between Meditation and Reduced (Brain) Aging: An Attempt to Bridge Some Gaps between the Alleged Fountain of Youth and the Youth of the Field," *Frontiers in Psychology* 8 (May 30, 2017): 860, https://doi.org/10.3389/fpsyg.2017.00860; Elizabeth A. Hoge, Maxine M. Chen, Esther Orr, Christina A. Metcalf, Laura E. Fischer, Mark H. Pollack, Immaculata De Vivo, and Naomi M. Simon, "Loving-Kindness Meditation Practice Associated with Longer Telomeres in Women," *Brain, Behavior, and Immunity* 32 (August 2013): 159–163; Manoj K. Bhasin, Jeffery A. Dusek, Bei-Hung Chang, Marie G. Joseph, John W. Denninger, Gregory L. Fricchione, Herbert Benson, and Towia A. Livermann, "Relaxation Response Induces Temporal Transcriptome Changes in Energy Metabolism, Insulin Secretion and Inflammatory Pathways," *PLoS ONE* 8, 5 (May 1, 2013): e62817, https:// doi.org/10.1371/journal.pone.0062817; Eileen Luders, Florian Kurth, Emeran A. Mayer, Arthur W. Toga, Katherine L. Narr, and Christian Gaser, "The Unique Brain Anatomy of Meditation Practitioners: Alterations in Cortical Gyrification, *Frontiers in Human Neuroscience* 6 (February 29, 2012): 34, https://doi.org/10.3389/fnhum.2012.00034; David S. Black and George M. Slavich, "Mindfulness Meditation and the Immune

System: A Systematic Review of Randomized Controlled Trials," *Annals of the New York Academy of Sciences*, 1373, 1 (January 21, 2016): 13–24, https://doi.org/10.1111/nyas.12998.

8 Flower A. Newhouse, *Natives of Eternity* (Vista, CA: Lawrence G. Newhouse, 1950), 26.

9 Black Elk as quoted by Fools Crow, in Mails, *Fools Crow*, 30.

10 Mails, *Fools Crow*, 30.

11 Mails, *Fools Crow*, 36.

12 Joyce Elaine Noll, *Company of Prophets: African American Psychics, Healers, and Visionaries* (New York: Llewellyn; 2nd Print edition, January 1, 1992), 138. In many of his books, Shealy tells the story of meeting Rucker and being introduced through him to the whole concept of medical intuition. See, for example, Caroline Myss and C. Norman Shealy, *The Creation of Health: The Emotional, Psychological, and Spiritual Responses That Promote Health and Healing* (Potter, 1998). For more about Rucker, see Hans Holzer, *Beyond Medicine: The Facts about Unorthodox and Psychic Healing* (Chicago: Henry Regnery Company, 1973) and Brad Steiger, *Psychic City: Chicago: Doorway to Another Dimension* (Garden City, NY: Doubleday, 1976).

13 Noll, *Company of Prophets*, 39.

14 Choquette, *Diary of a Psychic*, 108.

15 Dowoti Désir, "Vodou: A Sacred Multidimensional, Pluralistic Space," *Teaching Theology and Religion* 9, no. 2 (April 2006): 91–96.

CHAPTER 6

1 See Dolores Cannon's discussion of vacation lives in her five-book series, *The Convoluted Universe* (Huntsville, AR: Ozark Mountain Publishing, 2001–2015).

2 See for example, Robert Schwartz, *Courageous Souls: Do We Plan Our Life Challenges Before Birth?* 2nd ed. (Chesterland, OH: Whispering Winds Press; 2006).

3 Dannion Brinkley, *Saved by the Light: The True Story of a Man Who Died Twice and the Profound Revelations He Received* (New York: Villard Books, 1994), 119.

4 John Holland, *Born Knowing*, 2nd ed. (Carlsbad, CA: Hay House, 2003), 40.

5 John Edward, *Infinite Quest: Develop Your Psychic Intuition to Take Charge of Your Life* (New York: Sterling, 210), 232–33.

6 Michelle Kahn-John and Mary Koithan, "Living in Health, Harmony, and Beauty: The Diné (Navajo) Hózhó Wellness Philosophy," *Global Advances in Health and Medicine*, 4, no. 3 (May 2015): 24–30.

INDEX

A

access to service, setting pricing, 150
accuracy
    ethical ramifications, 31–33
    giving refunds, 124–126
    guarantees, 150
    not overpromising, 149
adulterous affairs, 60, 61, 94–95, 123
advice of elders, 105
affirmations, 70
African Americans
    cultural appropriation, 19–21
    cultural denial and rediscovery,
        25, 26
    Hoodoo. See Hoodoo
Akashic Records, 4, 5, 13, 63, 72,
    94, 106
    privacy issues, 50–51
alcoholism/addiction
    being sensitive to client needs, 36
    self-awareness, 30
    spirit attachment, 98
ancestors, listening to, 42
angels and archangels, 100–101
answering questions about people
    not present, 123–124
apprenticeships, 2, 104, 148
Association of Independent Readers
    and Rootworkers (AIRR), 56–57
astral beings
    sending to the light, 133–136
    summoning, 42
astral plane connections, 78, 110

authenticity, 13–29
    cultural appropriation, 17–23,
        28–29
    culture sharing, 23–28
    mediums, 14–17
automatic writing, 43

B

bad news, risk of making matters
    worse, 58–64
balance, 37, 120, 121, 122
balanced living, 115–116
Baron-Reid, Colette, 53
becoming a hollow bone, 112–115
becoming an ethical psychic
    becoming a hollow bone,
        112–115
    choosing colleagues, 107
    choosing teachers, 103–106
    doing emotional work, 108–112
    examining your motives, 107–108
    living a balanced life, 115–116
beginning psychics. See also
    students
    training, 2–3
    usefulness of this book, 4–5
being authentic, 13–29
    cultural appropriation, 17–23,
        28–29
    culture sharing, 23–28
    mediums, 14–17
being humble, 31–36

being of service, 37
being self-aware, 29–31
being sensitive to client needs, 36–40
Bikram Choudhury, 85
Billy, Danny, 105
binding, 42
Black Elk, 112–113
black magicians vs. white
    magicians, 3
Black Native American Association
    of Oakland, 6
Black Spiritualist churches, 6
Bojack, 6
Brown, Peter, 114
Brujeria, 67, 107
    historical context, 68–69
Buenaflor, Erika, 24–25, 69

C

cancer patients, 60, 61, 62–64
candle petitions (valaciónes), 69–70
Cannon, Dolores, 6
Cassadaga Spiritualist Camp, 6
Catches, Peter S., 1
Cayce, Edgar, 70-71
Cereclasses, 21–22
ceremonies, 102
chakras, sexual energy, 74–76, 84
chambers of commerce, 104
Chamiel the archangel, 100
character. *See* traits of ethical psychics
charity, 140, 150
Chauran, Alexandra, 48, 52, 104
cheating spouse/partner, 60, 61,
    94–95, 123
choosing colleagues, 107
choosing teachers, 103–106
Choquette, Sonia, 104, 114–115
clients
    being sensitive to client needs,
        36–40
    cutting cords, 132–133
    danger, 61–62, 64

dating, 116, 131
dependency, 51–55, 126–127
family members, 130–131
financial exploitation, 55–58
making matters worse, 58–64
refunds, 124–126
refusing to work with certain
    clients, 126–130
coaching, 104–105
colleagues
    choosing, 107
    feedback from, 141–142
Conjure, 67–68. *See also* Hoodoo
continuing education, 104–105
controlling destiny of souls, 90–96
cords, cutting, 132–133
core shamanism, 18
Council of American Witches, 66
counseling, 104–105
Creator, 41, 44
criticism, accepting, 36
cults, 85–87
cultural appropriation, 17–23, 28–29
    African and African American
        culture, 19–21
    ethics of magic and witchcraft, 67
    examples of, 23
    fake gurus, 81
    Harnerism, 18–19
    respecting other's traditions,
        22–23
    sound healing, 19
    term "shaman", 17–18
    Wicca/witchcraft, 21
culture sharing, 23–28
curandera, 24
curanderismo, 24
cutting cords, 132–133

D

danger, 61–62, 64
Dannion Brinkley, 139
dating clients, 116, 131

Davenport, Don Little Cloud, 6
demons, 44, 133–136
dependency, clients, 51–55,
   126–127
depressed clients, 61
destiny of souls, controlling, 90–96
devas, 100
diagnosing illness, 144–145
Diary of a Psychic (Choquette),
   114–115
disease, 117–119
divorce, 117–119
doing emotional work, 108–112
dreams, 78, 110
drug use by supersensory
   persons, 102
DuBois, Allison, 14, 64
dying clients, 117–119

E

earthbound spirits, 44, 96–100
   sending to the light, 133–136
Edward, John, 13, 66, 143
ego, 113–115
elders, 105
egregore, binding, 42
Embry, Zenobia, 6
emotional dependency of clients,
   51–55, 126–127
emotional inventories, 112
emotional proclivities and wounds,
   self-awareness, 30–31
emotional work, 108–112
energy healers, 4
   misuse of sexual energy, 74–79
ESP, 1
ethical psychic
   definition of, 3
   traits of. *See* traits of ethical
      psychics
   usefulness of this book, 4–5
ethics, 67
examining your motives, 107–108

expectations, setting, 52
exploitation of clients, financially,
   55–58
extramarital affairs, 60, 61, 94–95, 123

F

fake gurus and shamans, 80–88
   cults, 86–87
   cultural appropriation, 81
   sex abuse, 84
   traits of true gurus, 81–82
family members, reading for,
   130–131
fees, 146–150
   setting, 57–58
financial exploitation of clients,
   55–58
Fools Crow, 9, 65, 103, 113
foretelling the future, 95, 137–138
Foundation for Shamanic Studies, 18
fraud, 56
   fake gurus and shamans, 80–88
   financial exploitation of clients,
      55–58
free will, 66, 70, 72, 79, 95, 97–98
future, predicting, 95, 137–138

G

Gabriel the archangel, 100
Geller, Uri, 29
giving refunds, 124–126
God
   angels and archangels, 100–101
   listening to a higher source,
      40–41, 44
   not disregarding guidance/
      feedback from humans,
      141–142
The Great I Am, 44
grief, 15, 37, 64, 91, 93
guarantees, 150

"Guruji", 85
gurus
    fake, 80–88
    traits of true gurus, 81–82

H

Hall of Records, 94. *See also* Akashic
    Records
Hall, Manly P., 3, 73–74
hallucinogen use, 102
Harner, Michael, 18–19
Harnerism, 18–19
healers
    mentally ill clients, 144
    misuse of sexual energy,
        74–79
    sending entities to the light,
        133–136
helicopter parents, 123–124
herbalists' cultural appropriation of
    Hoodoo, 20
hexes, 69
Higher Self, 44
higher source
    listening to, 40–45
    not disregarding guidance/
        feedback from humans,
        141–142
Hippocrates, 73
Holland, John, 104, 141
hollow bone, becoming, 112–115
Hoodoo, 5, 7, 67–69
    Association of Independent
        Readers and Rootworkers
        (AIRR), 56–57
    Code of Ethics, 105
    cultural appropriation, 20, 21
    historical context, 68–69
    spellbooks, 67
Hoskie, Don, 82
humility, 31–36
    remaining open to advice and
        guidance, 142

Hurston, Zora Neale, 67–68
hypocrisy, fake gurus, 86

I

ignorance, 74
illness
    diagnosing, 144–145
    mentally ill clients, 143–144
    risk of making matters worse,
        60–64
Indigenous peoples
    character, 9
    cultural appropriation, 27–28
    cultural denial and rediscovery,
        25–26
    psychic training, 2
    seeking advice of elders, 105
    shamans, 82–83
    support of medicine people, 146
Inspirational Writing, 43–44
interdimensional beings, binding, 42
intimacy, 116
invasion of privacy, risk of, 48–51

J

Jamaican Revivalism, 5
James, Jesse, Jr., 11
jinns, 42, 44
Joho, Jess, 21
joining professional organizations, 104

K

karma, 120–122
    contracts, 93
    debts, 73
    misuse of sexual energy, 79
    repercussions of what you do
        and say, 13
Kecheshawno, Millie, 6

L

Leadbetter, Charles W., 89
learning from mistakes, 31–33
listening to a higher source,
    40–45
living a balanced life, 115–116
Lord Acton, 87
love triangles, 94
Lula-Mae, 5

M

magic
    ethics, 66–67
    ignorance, 74
    opening portals, 101–102
magick, 107
    listening to a higher
        source, 42
making matters worse, 58–64
Manci, Mercy, 58
Maseko, Nhlonono, 42
Master Choa, 6
Mayeng, Isaac, 40
medical intuitives, 4, 5, 60
    being self-aware, 30
    diagnosing illness,
        144–145
    Edgar Cayce, 70–71
medicine people, 75
meditation, 111–112
mediums, 4
    authenticity, 14–17
    being self-aware, 30
    importance of working
        with a Higher Power,
        43–44
    platform mediumship, 16
    possession and earthbound
        spirits, 96–100
    sending entities to the light,
        133–136
    spirit attachment, 97–98
Meley, Chloé, 20

mental illness, 83–84, 92, 129,
    143–144
    client dependency, 53–54
Metatron the archangel, 100
Michael the archangel, 100
mind-knowers, 49
mind-pickers, 49
mistakes, learning from, 31–33
misuse of sexual energy, 74–79
    fake gurus, 80–88
Mother Barrett, 5
Mother Joyce, 5
Mother Mavis, 5
Mother Robinson, 5
Mother Viola, 5
Mother Wright, 5
motivation
    examining your motives,
        107–108
    service, 11–13
    white magicians vs. black
        magicians, 3
murder victims, 64

N

Native Americans. *See also*
    Indigenous peoples
    cultural denial and rediscovery,
        25, 26
    sweat lodges, 5–6
Newhouse, Flower, 112
Nohavec, Janet, 47

O

Orishas, 14
    Santeros Against Fraud and
        Exploitation (SAFE),
        56–57
Other World, 5, 89, 96–98, 137
Ouija board, 136–137
overpromising, 149

P

past lives, 94–95, 121–122
perverting the will of another, 65–74
    fake gurus, 80–88
Phoenix Bennett, 6
platform mediumship, 16
portals, 100–102
possession, 96–100
power
    cults, 86–87
    ego, 114
    fake gurus and shamans, 80–88
    misuse of sexual energy, 74–79
    perverting the will of another,
        65–74
    risk of abuse, 65
    seductive effects of, 87–88
Pranic Healing, 5–6
precognition, 95, 137–138
Presley, Elvis, 20
pricing
    financial exploitation of clients,
        55–58
    setting, 57–58, 146–150
privacy
    Akashic Records, 50–51
    answering questions about
        other people, 50
    mind-picking, 49
    sensitivity to client needs, 38
privacy invasion, 48–51
professional organizations, 104
prophecies, 95, 137–138
psychic detectives, 30
psychics. See also ethical psychic
    sexual attraction, 76–77
    training in Indigenous cultures, 2
    unethical, 1

Q

quantum healing hypnosis
    technique (QHHT), 5, 6

Queenie, 5
Questhaven Retreat, 112

R

racism, 69
random spontaneous readings,
    138–141
Ray, James Arthur, 85
reading for family members,
    130–131
refunds, 124–126
refusing to work with certain
    clients, 126–130
Reiki, 5–6, 75
relationships
    adulterous affairs, 60, 61,
        94–95, 123
    dating clients, 116, 131
    helicopter parents, 123–124
Revivalism, 5
Rey, Freya, 32
risks, 47–64
    client dependency, 51–55,
        126–127
    controlling destiny of souls,
        90–96
    creating disharmony through
        portals and possession,
        96–102
    financial exploitation, 55–58
    invasion of privacy, 48–51
    making matters worse,
        58–64
    perverting will of another,
        66–74
    misuse of sexual energy,
        74–88
Rootwork. See also Hoodoo
    Association of Independent
        Readers and Rootworkers
        (AIRR), 56–57
    cultural appropriation, 20
Rucker, Henry, 113

S

Sangoma, 41–42
Santeros Against Fraud and
    Exploitation (SAFE), 56–57
Sedona, Arizona, 101
self-awareness, 29–31, 110
sending entities to the light,
    133–136
sensitivity to client needs, 36–40
service, 11–13
    being sensitive to client
        needs, 37
servitors, binding, 42
setting expectations, 52
setting prices, 146–150
sexual abuse
    fake gurus, 84
    misuse of sexual energy, 74–79
sexual energy
    misuse of, 74–79
    self-awareness, 30
shamans
    becoming a shaman, 82–83
    core shamanism, 18
    cultural appropriation of term
        "shaman", 17–18
    energy, 75
    fake shamans and gurus, 80–88
Shango, 5
Shealy Institute for Pain and Health
    Rehabilitation, 113
Shealy, Norman, 113
Shri K. Pattabhi Jois
    ("Guruji"), 85
Shri Mataji Nirmala Devi, 86
siddhis, 104
Sister Grant, 5
Sister Nelson, 5
Sizemore, Bonita, 6
slavery, 121
sobadoras, 75
soul paths, controlling destiny of
    souls, 89–96
sound healing, 19

Source
    listening to a higher source,
        40–41, 44
    not disregarding guidance/
        feedback from humans,
        141–142
spells
    casting, 69–72
    Hoodoo spellbooks, 67
    opening portals, 101–102
    removing, 133–135
Spirit
    listening to a higher source,
        40–41, 44
    not disregarding guidance/
        feedback from humans,
        141–142
spirit attachment, 97–98
spirit release work, 30
Spirit Teachers, 14
spirit vortex, 101
spirits, 89
    annoyance at being called down
        to Earth, 100
    controlling destiny of souls,
        90–96
    earthbound spirits, 96–100
    portals, 100–102
    sending to the light,
        133–136
    summoning, 42–43,
        136–137
spiritual healing, 5
spiritualism, 15
spontaneous readings, 138–141
students
    pricing during apprenticeship
        period, 148
    training, 2–3, 142–143
    usefulness of this book, 4–5
summoning spirits, 42–43
    impact on spirits, 136–137
Sung, Morgan, 21
Swami Satchidananda, 85
sweat lodges, 5–6

T

teachers
    choosing, 103–106
    usefulness of this book, 4
The Craft, 20, 67
thoughtforms, 133–135
three Ds, 117–119
Traditional Healers Organization
    (THO) of Africa, 42
training, 2–3, 142–143
traits of ethical psychics, 9–10
    Trait #1: Being of Service,
        11–13
    Trait #2: Being Authentic,
        13–29
    Trait #3: Being Self-Aware,
        29–31
    Trait #4: Learning from
        Mistakes and Being Humble,
        31–36
    Trait #5: Being Sensitive to
        Client Needs, 36–40
    Trait #6: Listening to a Higher
        Source, 40–45
traits of true gurus, 81–82
trauma, 111
Trinidadian Shango and
    spiritualism, 5

U

unethical risks, 47–48
    #1: Invading the Privacy of
        Others, 48–51
    #2: Client Dependency, 51–55
    #3: Financial Exploitation,
        55–58
    #4: Making Matters Worse,
        58–64

    #5: Perverting the Will of
        Another, 66–74
    #6: The Misuse of Sexual
        Energy, 74–88
    #7: Controlling the Destiny of
        Souls, 90–96
    #8: Creating Disharmony
        through Portals and
        Possession, 96–102
Universe, 44
unprocessed emotions, 109–111

V

valaciónes (candle petitions), 69–70
violet flame mantra, 135
Vodun, 67
Voodoo, 67–68
vortexes, 101

W

The Way of the Shaman (Harner), 18
Where Two Worlds Meet
    (Nohavec), 47
white magicians vs. black
    magicians, 3
Wicca
    cultural appropriation, 21
    ethics, 66-67
    summoning, 42
will
    of psychics, 1
    perverting the will of another,
        65–74
witchcraft
    cultural appropriation, 21
    ethics, 66-67
witches' rede, 66

ABOUT THE AUTHOR

JENNIFER LISA VEST is a scientist-philosopher-intuitive. She holds a PhD in Indigenous Philosophy from UC Berkeley, an MA in history from Howard, and BA in Physics from Hampshire College. Her first career was as a philosophy professor at Seattle University and the University of Central Florida. Spiritually, Vest is a medical intuitive and an Akashic Records reader, is certified as a Quantum Healing Hypnosis Technique practitioner and a Master Reiki practitioner, and has been trained in the traditions of African American Hoodoo, Native American sweat lodge, Jamaican Revivalism, Trinidadian Shango, and spiritualism from community elders.

About North Atlantic Books

North Atlantic Books (NAB) is a 501(c)(3) nonprofit publisher committed to a bold exploration of the relationships between mind, body, spirit, culture, and nature. Founded in 1974, NAB aims to nurture a holistic view of the arts, sciences, humanities, and healing. To make a donation or to learn more about our books, authors, events, and newsletter, please visit www.northatlanticbooks.com.